Vlad the Impaler
Fear, Power and Control

A.A. Castor

Table of Contents

Vlad the Impaler: Fear, Power and Control

A.A. Castor

Dedication

To my beloved family,

Your unconditional love, unwavering support, and endless encouragement have been my greatest blessings. From the earliest days of dreaming to the challenging moments of writing, you have stood by me with patience and belief. This book is as much yours as it is mine, a reflection of the values you've instilled and the faith you've shown in me. Thank you for being my rock and my inspiration.

To my dear friends,

Your friendship has illuminated my path with laughter, shared moments, and invaluable support. You've cheered me on through every triumph and lifted me up through every challenge. Your belief in my endeavors has been a source of strength and motivation. This book is a testament to the power of friendship, and I am grateful for each of you who has walked this journey by my side.

To God,

Your grace and guidance have been my constant companions. In moments of doubt, you've shown me the way; in moments of joy, you've multiplied my gratitude. This book is a testament to your faithfulness and the blessings you've bestowed upon me. May it serve as a reflection of your love and the lessons you continue to teach me.

With heartfelt gratitude and love,

A.A. Castor

Copyright © 2024 by A.A. Castor

Philippine Copyright Law:

Why I Am Writing This Book

Throughout history, few figures have sparked as much **fear, fascination**, and **controversy** as Vlad the Impaler. Known for his **ruthless leadership** and **brutal tactics**, Vlad's reign offers a unique lens through which to explore the complex dynamics of **power, fear, and control**. As a writer and researcher with a deep passion for **history and leadership**, I was drawn to Vlad not just for his notorious reputation, but for the **leadership lessons** hidden beneath the surface of his often terrifying legacy.

This book is not a glorification of **brutality** or **authoritarian rule**, but an **examination** of the circumstances that shaped Vlad's approach to leadership and governance. My goal is to explore how his use of **fear as a tool** of control, his decisive actions in moments of crisis, and his ability to maintain power in a politically unstable region can offer **insights** for modern leaders. By understanding his methods—both the strengths and the flaws—we can extract **timeless lessons** that are applicable in today's world, whether in leadership, governance, or personal development.

I also want to challenge the **mythical narrative** surrounding Vlad the Impaler, particularly his association with the fictional Dracula. While the legend is intriguing, I believe it's important to separate **fact from fiction** and examine Vlad's leadership style in the context of the **political, social**, and **military challenges** of his time. By doing so, I hope to provide a more nuanced understanding of a leader who used extreme measures to achieve his goals, while also highlighting the **consequences of ruling through fear.**

Ultimately, this book aims to shed light on the **complexity of leadership**, showing that even the most ruthless figures have lessons to teach. By reflecting on Vlad's reign, we can better understand the balance between **strength, morality**, and **the long-term impact** of leadership decisions.

Warning and Disclaimer

The information provided in this book is intended for educational and informational purposes only. While every effort has been made to ensure the accuracy and reliability of the content, the author and publisher make no representations or warranties regarding the completeness, accuracy, or applicability of the information presented. The strategies, insights, and historical examples discussed are based on personal interpretations and research and may not be universally applicable in all situations.

The author and publisher disclaim any liability for any loss, damage, or inconvenience arising from the use of the information in this book. Readers are encouraged to exercise their own judgment and seek professional advice when applying the lessons, strategies, or concepts discussed herein to their own personal or professional circumstances.

Neither the author nor the publisher shall be held liable for any direct or indirect consequences resulting from the use or misuse of the material presented in this book.

About the Author

A.A. Castor is a dedicated writer and researcher, with a focus on uncovering timeless leadership strategies from some of history's most fascinating figures. In this book, Castor delves deep into the life and legacy of **Vlad the Impaler**, analyzing the complex and often brutal leadership methods that shaped his reign. Castor's passion for **leadership, history, and strategy** shines through in his work, blending historical analysis with **modern-day applications** to offer practical insights for today's leaders.

Known for his ability to bridge the gap between **historical wisdom** and contemporary leadership challenges, Castor explores topics ranging from **political strategy and governance** to **social dynamics and power**. His writing offers readers compelling narratives while providing **actionable lessons** that can be applied in both personal and professional contexts.

Inspired by historical figures such as **Augustus Caesar** and **Vlad the Impaler**, Castor's work seeks to uncover the **tactical brilliance** and **strategic thinking** behind some of the most influential leaders in history. His background in **historical study** and **leadership theory** informs his research, making his books not only informative but deeply relevant to modern leadership challenges.

When not writing, A.A. Castor enjoys hosting podcasts on **leadership, history**, and **social philosophy**, continuing his mission to bring historical lessons into the present day.

Introduction: The Man Behind the Myth

Overview of Vlad the Impaler's Life and Reign

Vlad III, also known as **Vlad the Impaler** and **Vlad Dracula**, was born in 1431 in Transylvania, then part of the Kingdom of Hungary. He was a member of the House of Drăculești, a branch of the House of Basarab, and the son of Vlad II Dracul. His early life was marked by political instability, as Wallachia, his homeland, was a battleground between the Ottoman Empire and Christian Europe.

At a young age, Vlad and his brother Radu were held as political hostages by the Ottomans, where Vlad witnessed brutal tactics and strategies that would later influence his own leadership. Upon returning to Wallachia, he embarked on a quest to secure his throne and defend his principality against both internal rivals and the Ottoman threat.

Vlad's reign is best remembered for his ruthless methods of maintaining order and deterring enemies, earning him the moniker "Vlad the Impaler" due to his practice of impaling thousands of enemies on stakes. This form of extreme punishment served not only as a method of execution but also as a psychological weapon, instilling fear in both domestic traitors and foreign adversaries.

His most notable military campaign occurred in 1462, when he led a fierce resistance against the Ottoman Sultan Mehmed II. Although vastly outnumbered, Vlad's use of guerrilla tactics, including the infamous "Night Attack," managed to inflict heavy losses on the Ottoman forces, demonstrating his prowess in asymmetric warfare.

Despite his successes, Vlad's rule was marred by political intrigue and betrayal. He was deposed and imprisoned several times during his life, eventually losing the throne for good. He was killed in battle in 1476, but his legacy lived on, particularly through the folklore that later inspired Bram Stoker's *Dracula*.

Vlad's reign, while characterized by extreme cruelty, was also marked by efforts to strengthen Wallachia's autonomy, reduce crime, and stabilize the region in the face of overwhelming external threats. To this day, he remains a complex figure: a hero to some for defending his homeland from Ottoman invasion, and a symbol of tyranny and terror to others.

Clarifying the Distinction Between Vlad the Impaler and the Dracula Myth

WHILE **Vlad the Impaler** was a historical figure, his name and legacy became intertwined with the fictional character of **Count Dracula**, largely due to Bram Stoker's 1897 novel *Dracula*. It's important to distinguish between the reality of Vlad's life and reign, and the fictional vampire legend that grew out of it.

Vlad the Impaler, or **Vlad III of Wallachia**, was a 15th-century ruler known for his brutal methods of maintaining control, including his notorious practice of impaling his enemies. His reign was marked by relentless battles against internal rivals and the advancing Ottoman Empire, where he demonstrated cunning, fear, and strategic ruthlessness. His harsh rule, often viewed as a necessary evil in the defense of his land, also earned him a fearsome reputation in Europe.

Count Dracula, on the other hand, is a fictional vampire created by Bram Stoker. The character is an undead aristocrat who feeds on the blood of the living, with many traits drawn from European vampire folklore. Stoker is believed to have drawn inspiration from Vlad the Impaler, using his moniker "Dracula" (which means "son of the dragon" or "son of the devil" in Romanian) for the fictional count. However, the vampire's supernatural abilities and thirst for blood are entirely fictional and have no basis in Vlad's actual life.

The **myth of Dracula** has often overshadowed the real historical achievements and horrors of Vlad the Impaler, reducing him to a mere villain in popular culture. However, Vlad was primarily a military leader and ruler, not a mythical creature. His use of terror as a tool of governance, while extreme, was part of a strategy to protect Wallachia from foreign invaders and ensure political stability in a volatile era.

This distinction is crucial for understanding the complexity of Vlad's historical legacy. While the Dracula myth thrives in literature and entertainment, the real Vlad III was a powerful, albeit brutal, leader who navigated the challenges of his time with a focus on power, control, and survival.

Setting the Tone: Understanding Vlad's Use of Fear, Power, and Control as Leadership Tools

AT THE HEART OF THIS book lies an exploration of **Vlad the Impaler's strategic use of fear, power, and control** as essential tools in his leadership. Far from being a mindless tyrant, Vlad's harsh methods were calculated and driven by necessity, shaped by the turbulent political and military landscape of 15th-century Eastern Europe. His story is not just one of cruelty but of survival in a world where leaders had to be as feared as they were respected to maintain authority.

Vlad's leadership style was forged in a time when Wallachia faced constant threats from external forces—particularly the expanding Ottoman Empire—and internal instability. Surrounded by enemies and rivals, Vlad needed to impose absolute control over his territory to secure his rule and protect his people. In this context, **fear became his greatest weapon.** By employing terrifying punishments like impalement, Vlad instilled discipline among his subjects and sent a clear message to his enemies: rebellion and disloyalty would be met with unimaginable consequences.

But fear alone wasn't enough. Vlad combined his reputation for ruthlessness with strategic brilliance and political cunning. **Power** wasn't just about terror; it was about calculated military actions, psychological warfare, and diplomatic maneuvers. His ability to outwit larger and better-equipped armies with unconventional tactics, such as guerrilla warfare and surprise attacks, showcased his mastery of warfare. His alliances and betrayals further demonstrated a deep understanding of political power, knowing when to strike and when to negotiate.

In Vlad's world, **control** was crucial to survival. His severe laws and methods of justice were designed to keep a fractured and divided Wallachia united under his reign. Maintaining control over his nobility, ensuring loyalty from his people, and guarding against foreign influence required decisive and, often, brutal measures.

This book will delve into how **Vlad's use of fear, power, and control** allowed him to secure and sustain his rule, even in the face of overwhelming odds. While his tactics may seem extreme by modern standards, they offer timeless lessons in leadership, strategy, and the balancing act of maintaining authority in volatile circumstances. Vlad's legacy shows that fear, when wielded wisely, can be an essential tool for leaders seeking to establish order in times of chaos.

Chapter 1: The Making of Vlad the Impaler

Vlad the Impaler's rise to power did not happen in a vacuum. His brutal reputation and infamous methods of control were the product of a life marked by hardship, betrayal, and violence. Born into a noble family in the politically unstable region of Wallachia, Vlad's early years were shaped by a fierce struggle for survival. He was thrust into a world where shifting alliances, internal treachery, and external threats from empires like the Ottomans and the Hungarians were constant realities.

The boy who would grow into the fearsome leader known as Vlad the Impaler was shaped by the turbulence of his time. The violent deaths of his father and brother, his years spent as a hostage in the Ottoman Empire, and the constant threat of betrayal at the hands of the Wallachian boyars all contributed to his hardened outlook on power and control. These formative experiences would become the foundation for his notorious reign, where fear, brutality, and a relentless quest for stability defined his leadership.

At the heart of Vlad's evolution was the intense pressure to navigate a complex political landscape. Wallachia was caught between two powerful empires—the **Ottoman Empire**, which sought to extend its dominance into Europe, and the **Kingdom of Hungary**, a Christian bulwark against the Muslim Ottomans. Wallachian princes, including Vlad's father, Vlad II Dracul, constantly had to balance their allegiances, shifting between appeasing the Ottomans and seeking Hungarian support to retain their fragile hold on power. For young

Vlad, this meant learning at an early age that trust was fleeting and that survival depended on ruthless decisiveness.

His time spent as a **hostage of the Ottomans** added another layer to his psychological development. Vlad was not only exposed to the ruthless methods of the Ottoman rulers, but also to the complexities of power dynamics at the imperial court. He witnessed the effectiveness of fear as a tool of control—an impression that would deeply influence his future leadership style. The experience of living under the watchful eye of his captors, knowing that his life depended on his father's political decisions, imbued him with a sense of suspicion and caution that would shape his rule in Wallachia.

Beyond political survival, personal betrayal deeply scarred Vlad. The murder of his father and elder brother at the hands of his family's rivals left an indelible mark on him. The boyars who had betrayed his family became the target of his later rage and retribution. Vlad's brutal treatment of these nobles was not just an act of revenge, but a clear demonstration of his belief that fear and power were the only reliable means to maintain loyalty and control.

This chapter delves into **Vlad's formative years**, illustrating how the turbulent political climate, his personal losses, and his time as a hostage coalesced to create the ruthless leader history remembers. These early experiences set the stage for the man who would become known for his merciless tactics, using brutality as a form of governance and fear as the cornerstone of his power. It was in these years that Vlad learned that mercy was a weakness, and in his world, only the strong could survive.

Vlad's Early Life, His Family, and the Political Environment of Wallachia

VLAD III, LATER KNOWN as **Vlad the Impaler**, was born in 1431 in **Sighişoara, Transylvania**, into the House of Drăculeşti, a prominent family in Wallachia. His father, **Vlad II Dracul**, was a member of the **Order of the Dragon**, a Christian chivalric order founded to defend Europe against the Ottoman Empire. The title "Dracul," meaning "the Dragon" or "the Devil" in Romanian, was inherited by Vlad III, giving him the moniker "Dracula," or "son of the Dragon."

Family Background

Vlad III was the second of four brothers, with **Radu the Handsome** and **Mircea II** being the most notable among them. His upbringing was deeply influenced by the political struggles of the time. His father, Vlad II Dracul, became **Voivode (Prince) of Wallachia** in 1436, but his rule was anything but stable. Wallachia, a small principality caught between two powerful empires—**the Ottoman Empire to the south** and **the Kingdom of Hungary to the north**—was a region of constant conflict and shifting alliances.

Ottoman Influence and Hostage Years

In 1442, as part of his political dealings to maintain peace with the Ottomans, Vlad II sent his sons **Vlad III** and **Radu** as hostages to the Ottoman court. Vlad III spent his formative years in **Adrianople** and later in **Tokat**, where he was held by the Ottomans as a guarantee of his father's loyalty. During this time, Vlad witnessed the inner workings of the Ottoman court, learned Turkish, and became well-versed in Ottoman military tactics and political strategies. The psychological toll of being a hostage, combined with the brutality he saw, likely shaped his future ruthlessness.

This period also exposed Vlad to contrasting influences: while his brother Radu became closely aligned with the Ottomans, eventually converting to Islam and serving in the Ottoman military, Vlad III developed a deep resentment toward his captors. This animosity would fuel his fierce resistance against Ottoman expansion in later years.

Wallachia's Political Turmoil

Wallachia itself was a land of constant political instability. The region was under perpetual threat from the **Ottoman Empire**, which sought to expand its territory into Europe. At the same time, Wallachian rulers had to manage precarious relationships with **Hungary** and **Transylvania**, seeking protection from Christian powers while avoiding complete subjugation by the Ottomans. The **boyars** (noble families) of Wallachia further complicated the political landscape, often plotting against their rulers, including Vlad's father, to gain power for themselves.

Vlad II Dracul's loyalty to the Ottomans and his failure to decisively choose between the Ottoman Sultan and the Hungarian King weakened his position. This indecisiveness would eventually lead to his downfall and death in 1447, when he and his eldest son, Mircea, were assassinated by rival boyars.

Early Influences and the Desire for Revenge

Following the murder of his father and brother, Vlad III harbored a **burning desire for revenge** against the boyars who betrayed his family and against the foreign powers that manipulated Wallachia's politics. Upon his return to Wallachia in 1456, after gaining support from Hungary, Vlad embarked on a mission not only to reclaim his father's throne but also to exact brutal retribution on those who had wronged him.

This early chapter of Vlad's life, shaped by betrayal, captivity, and political chaos, forged him into the ruthless leader he would become. His childhood experiences in the Ottoman Empire and the tragic fate of his family provided him with a deep understanding of both the complexities of political power and the necessity of ruthless control. These experiences set the stage for his reign, during which he would use **fear, power, and control** to solidify his position as one of the most infamous rulers in European history.

His time as a hostage of the Ottoman Empire and the lessons he learned

IN 1442, AS PART OF a political arrangement to secure his loyalty to the Ottoman Empire, Vlad's father, Vlad II Dracul, sent both Vlad III and his younger brother Radu to the Ottoman court as hostages. This was a common practice at the time, designed to ensure that rulers like Vlad's father would remain compliant with Ottoman demands. Vlad and Radu were taken to **Adrianople** (modern-day Edirne) and later to **Tokat**, where they spent several years under the watchful eye of the Ottoman Sultan.

During his captivity, **Vlad was exposed to the harsh realities of Ottoman rule**. He witnessed firsthand the Ottoman Empire's brutal military tactics and its strict approach to governance. The **Ottomans ruled through fear and dominance**, often employing cruel punishments to maintain control over their vast territories. Vlad would have observed how the empire kept rebellious regions in line and how military power was leveraged to expand their influence. These observations made a lasting impression on him and would later influence his own ruthless methods of rule in Wallachia.

The psychological toll of captivity also played a significant role in shaping Vlad's character. Though treated relatively well by his captors, Vlad was essentially a political prisoner, living far from his homeland and constantly aware of the precarious position he and his family were in. His brother Radu adapted more easily to the Ottomans, even converting to Islam and serving as a trusted soldier under the Sultan. Vlad, however, developed a deep **resentment** toward his captors, which would later fuel his **lifelong animosity toward the Ottoman Empire**.

During his time in the Ottoman court, Vlad was also **educated in warfare, politics, and diplomacy**. The Ottomans, a formidable military force, imparted lessons in the art of war, tactics that Vlad would later use in his guerrilla campaigns against them. He became familiar with **Ottoman military strategies**, including the importance of swift, decisive attacks and the use of terror to demoralize opponents. These lessons in **psychological warfare** were particularly influential, and Vlad would later employ them to devastating effect in his infamous Night Attack on the Ottomans.

In addition to military tactics, Vlad learned about **political strategy** from the Ottoman court. He observed how the Sultan maintained control over a diverse empire through a combination of diplomatic alliances, strategic marriages, and ruthless enforcement of power. These lessons in **ruthless governance** would later inspire Vlad's own uncompromising approach to rule, as he used similar methods to quell dissent and maintain order in Wallachia.

Ultimately, **Vlad's time as a hostage** provided him with a unique blend of knowledge and bitterness. He came to **understand the value of fear** in governance, recognizing that terror could be an effective means of consolidating power and maintaining control. Upon his return to Wallachia, he would put these lessons into practice, using fear not only to defend his throne but also to create an enduring legacy of power and authority.

The factors that shaped his ruthless approach to leadership

VLAD THE IMPALER'S brutal approach to leadership was shaped by a combination of personal experiences, political instability, and cultural influences. His early exposure to **betrayal and violence**, combined with the constant threat to his family's rule, contributed significantly to his harsh methods of governance.

One of the most critical factors was **the betrayal of his father and older brother**. In 1447, his father, Vlad II Dracul, was overthrown and killed by rival noble factions in Wallachia, and his older brother, Mircea, was tortured and buried alive by these same boyars (nobles). This betrayal left a deep psychological scar on Vlad, instilling in him a **burning desire for revenge** against those who had wronged his family. The violent death of his father and brother at the hands of treacherous nobles would later justify his extreme punishment of Wallachian boyars, who he believed were inherently disloyal and corrupt.

Vlad's time as a **hostage in the Ottoman Empire** also shaped his outlook. He witnessed the Ottomans' use of **fear, intimidation, and cruelty** to maintain control over their vast empire. These lessons in the effectiveness of terror were deeply internalized, and Vlad came to view **fear as a necessary tool of leadership**. His experiences in captivity, combined with the betrayal of his family, reinforced his belief that **only through absolute control and the elimination of enemies** could a ruler maintain power and protect his kingdom.

Political instability in Wallachia was another significant factor. The region was a **constant battleground** between the Ottoman Empire and Hungary, with local nobles (boyars) frequently switching allegiances and plotting against their rulers. In such a volatile environment, Vlad realized that any show of weakness could result in his overthrow. His decision to rule with an iron fist was driven by the need to survive in a kingdom rife with treachery and external threats. His relentless crackdown on the boyars—whom he saw as disloyal and corrupt—was intended to break the cycle of betrayal and ensure **total loyalty** to his rule.

Vlad's **exposure to violence and war** from an early age also played a crucial role in shaping his leadership style. Growing up in a region where conflicts with the Ottomans were frequent, and witnessing brutal acts of war during his time in captivity, Vlad became desensitized to violence. He viewed cruelty not as an evil in itself, but as a **necessary means to an end**: the survival of his reign and the protection of Wallachia. His use of impalement, for which he became infamous, was not merely an act of sadism, but a calculated form of **psychological warfare** aimed at deterring enemies and keeping his subjects in line.

Finally, **Vlad's desire to restore order and stability** to Wallachia shaped his approach to leadership. Wallachia had long been a fragmented and unstable region, with weak rulers unable to control the boyars or defend the country from foreign powers. Vlad sought to **centralize power** and impose strict discipline on his subjects. His brutal enforcement of laws and punishments, including impalement for crimes like theft and disloyalty, was meant to create a sense of **fear and order** in a region that had been plagued by chaos.

In summary, **personal betrayal, political instability, exposure to Ottoman practices, and the desire for revenge and control** all shaped Vlad the Impaler's ruthless approach to leadership. His reign was defined by his belief that only through **fear, power, and absolute control** could he maintain order and protect his kingdom from internal and external threats.

Chapter 2: The Prince Returns

After years of exile and captivity, Vlad III made his way back to Wallachia, a land still in turmoil. His return was not a simple matter of reclaiming his father's throne—it was a battle against the very forces that had torn his family apart. Wallachia was a fragmented and vulnerable state, caught between the ambitions of the Ottoman Empire and the Kingdom of Hungary. The throne was a prize sought by many, and Vlad was determined to secure it, not only to restore his family's legacy but also to impose order on a land ravaged by betrayal and rebellion.

Vlad's return to Wallachia marked a turning point, not just for him personally, but for the entire region. His ascent to power would not come without bloodshed, and his path to the throne would be paved with the bodies of enemies, rivals, and traitors. But unlike other claimants, Vlad had learned valuable lessons from his time as a hostage. He understood that in a land plagued by instability, a ruler needed more than just claims of legitimacy; he needed to inspire fear and command respect.

When Vlad returned, Wallachia was divided, and the boyars—the noble class who had once betrayed his father—still held significant power. They were used to manipulating weak princes to their advantage, but Vlad had no intention of becoming their pawn. His claim to the throne was not just a bid for power; it was a declaration of revenge against the very forces that had torn his family apart. The boyars would soon learn that the prince who had returned was not the boy they once knew, but a man hardened by exile, captivity, and betrayal.

Vlad's journey back to power was marked by a ruthless strategy of eliminating rivals and consolidating control. He did not simply take the throne; he **seized it with calculated precision**. His vengeance against the boyars, who had played a role in his family's downfall, was swift and brutal. He would purge the ranks of his enemies through a series of **executions** and **mass impalements**, sending a clear message that disloyalty would no longer be tolerated in Wallachia.

In the eyes of his enemies, Vlad's actions may have seemed cruel and excessive, but for Vlad, they were necessary. Wallachia needed a strong, unquestioned ruler—someone who could repel foreign invaders and suppress internal rebellion. Vlad's return as prince was not about achieving short-term control; it was about establishing a long-lasting reign built on **unshakable authority**. He knew that fear, if used correctly, was a powerful tool that could unite a fractured state and deter foreign ambitions.

As he began to rebuild Wallachia, Vlad enacted a series of strict laws and punishments to maintain order, often relying on terror to enforce compliance. His reign was founded on the principle that **stability required brutality**, and that fear would inspire loyalty more effectively than mercy. Vlad's return to the throne, therefore, was more than a mere reclamation of his title—it was the beginning of a reign that would leave a permanent mark on history and earn him the fearsome title of Vlad the Impaler.

In this chapter, Vlad's transformation from a displaced prince to a ruler who would stop at nothing to control his realm unfolds. His return not only shaped his rule, but set the tone for the brutal tactics he would use to solidify his power and secure Wallachia's future amidst the chaos of medieval Europe. His reign, rooted in fear, power, and control, would become legendary, and the path to this dominance began the moment the prince returned.

Vlad's ascent to the throne of Wallachia

VLAD III'S PATH TO the throne of Wallachia was marked by turbulence, betrayal, and fierce determination. His initial claim to power came in 1448, but it was short-lived, lasting only a few months before he was ousted by rivals. This brief reign was the beginning of a long struggle to regain and hold onto his rightful place as voivode of Wallachia. During this time, Vlad was forced into exile, wandering through various courts in Eastern Europe and seeking alliances that would support his return to power.

Wallachia, strategically located between the **Ottoman Empire** and the **Kingdom of Hungary**, was a principality rife with political instability. The boyars, the ruling noble class, frequently shifted their loyalties between foreign powers and domestic claimants to the throne, creating a volatile environment in which power was never secure for long. Vlad's father, Vlad II Dracul, had experienced this instability firsthand, being forced to balance allegiance to the Ottomans with efforts to maintain independence. This delicate political landscape continued to haunt Wallachia after his father's death.

In 1456, after years of political maneuvering and exile, Vlad made a decisive move to reclaim his father's throne. With the backing of **John Hunyadi**, the powerful regent of Hungary, Vlad launched a campaign to retake Wallachia from his rival, Vladislav II, who had seized power during his absence. Unlike his first brief reign, this time Vlad was prepared for a long and bitter struggle. His return to Wallachia was not just about personal ambition but about restoring order to a fractured land and avenging the deaths of his father and brother.

Vlad's ascent to the throne was marked by his swift and **brutal consolidation of power**. Upon regaining control of Wallachia, he immediately set out to eliminate his rivals and secure his position. The boyars who had conspired against his father were among the first to face his wrath. He conducted a **bloody purge** of the nobility, executing or impaling those who had betrayed his family. This brutal act of vengeance not only avenged his father's death but also sent a clear message that disloyalty would not be tolerated under his rule.

Once his enemies within Wallachia were dealt with, Vlad turned his attention to the external threats facing his principality. The Ottoman Empire loomed large, and the Ottomans demanded tribute from Wallachia as a sign of submission. While his predecessors had tried to maintain a delicate balance with the Ottomans, Vlad refused to accept subjugation. Instead, he used **guerrilla warfare** and **psychological tactics** to challenge Ottoman advances, launching daring raids across the Danube and striking fear into the hearts of his enemies.

Vlad's rise to power was not simply a quest for a throne—it was a mission to reshape Wallachia. He wanted to transform it from a fragile state, constantly preyed upon by stronger powers, into a fortress of **unshakable authority**. His **uncompromising methods** in securing the throne laid the foundation for his reign, in which fear became his primary tool for maintaining control. By eliminating opposition both within and beyond Wallachia, Vlad cemented his place on the throne and created a legacy of power and terror that would echo through history.

The chaotic state of the region and how he seized control

IN THE MID-15TH CENTURY, Wallachia was a land beset by chaos. The principality was caught in the middle of a larger geopolitical struggle between two powerful empires—the **Ottoman Empire** to the south and the **Kingdom of Hungary** to the north. Both empires sought to control Wallachia, not only because of its strategic location but also because it served as a critical buffer zone in their ongoing conflicts. The internal dynamics of Wallachia itself were equally unstable, as the country was rife with power struggles between noble families, known as boyars, who often sought to influence or overthrow the ruling voivodes.

Wallachia's ruling class was divided, and alliances were constantly shifting. The boyars, with their wealth and influence, played a significant role in determining the fate of the throne, often conspiring with foreign powers or supporting rival claimants. As a result, the voivode's position was never secure for long, and betrayal was a common occurrence. This internal disunity made Wallachia vulnerable to both foreign invasion and civil strife.

By the time Vlad III sought to reclaim his father's throne in 1456, the situation had only worsened. His father, Vlad II Dracul, had been overthrown and murdered by Wallachian boyars, and Vlad himself had spent years in exile and captivity. The throne was now occupied by **Vladislav II**, a rival who had secured the boyars' backing and maintained an uneasy relationship with both Hungary and the Ottomans. In this fractured political landscape, Vlad III saw an opportunity to reclaim his birthright, but he knew that merely returning would not be enough. He would have to **seize control with brutal force** and dismantle the very system that had betrayed his family.

Vlad's return to Wallachia was marked by a carefully planned military campaign. With the support of **John Hunyadi**, the regent of Hungary, Vlad launched a decisive attack against Vladislav II, ultimately defeating him and reclaiming the throne. But Vlad's true genius lay in his ability to maintain control after his military victory. He understood that to rule effectively in such a chaotic environment, he had to **eliminate all internal threats** and make it clear that he would not tolerate the same betrayals that had plagued his father.

One of his first actions as ruler was to **purge the boyars**, the very class responsible for much of Wallachia's instability. Vlad viewed the boyars as a corrupt and treacherous group, and he believed that only through their complete subjugation or elimination could he establish a stable and loyal base of power. He began by inviting the boyars to a grand Easter feast in 1457. During the celebration, Vlad had many of the nobles executed on the spot, while others were forced into hard labor to build his fortress at **Poenari**. This purge sent a clear message that disloyalty would not be tolerated, and it effectively weakened the influence of the boyars, allowing Vlad to centralize power in his own hands.

Vlad also dealt with external threats with equal ruthlessness. Wallachia was expected to pay tribute to the Ottoman Empire, a demand that Vlad initially honored to secure his position. However, once his rule was firmly established, he openly defied the Ottomans, refusing to pay further tribute and launching a series of **bold raids across the Danube** into Ottoman territory. These raids, combined with Vlad's use of terror tactics like **impaling captured enemies**, created an aura of fear around him, further solidifying his control over Wallachia and discouraging foreign intervention.

Through his brutal and decisive actions, Vlad III was able to bring a degree of order to a region long plagued by chaos. By dismantling the power structures that had allowed for constant rebellion and foreign influence, he transformed Wallachia into a more centralized and controlled state. His reign, while brutal, was one of the few periods in Wallachian history where the throne was secure, and foreign invaders were held at bay. Vlad's ability to navigate the chaos of the region, and to seize control through fear, power, and strategic ruthlessness, is what ultimately allowed him to solidify his position as voivode of Wallachia.

Lessons in strategic thinking and capitalizing on opportunities in volatile situations

VLAD THE IMPALER'S rise to power was not just a matter of brute force; it was a testament to his **strategic thinking** and his ability to exploit the opportunities that arose in the chaotic political landscape of Wallachia. Surrounded by internal rivals and external threats, Vlad understood that survival required not only military prowess but also a deep understanding of when and how to act. His ascent to power and his reign offer valuable lessons in **capitalizing on instability**, using fear as a tool, and outmaneuvering opponents.

One of the key lessons from Vlad's strategy was his ability to **assess and exploit weaknesses** in both his enemies and his allies. When he returned to Wallachia, the region was rife with internal division, and the boyars—who had overthrown his father—remained a fractured and treacherous group. Vlad recognized that in such a volatile environment, there was an opportunity to **consolidate power by eliminating his most immediate internal threats**. Rather than attempting to negotiate or form alliances with the boyars, he saw that their disloyalty would eventually undermine him, as it had done to his father. His swift and brutal purge of the boyars was a calculated move to remove the power centers that could challenge his rule, allowing him to centralize authority in his own hands.

Another important aspect of Vlad's strategic thinking was his understanding of the **power of psychological warfare**. He knew that in a volatile situation, **fear could be as effective as military force** in controlling enemies and allies alike. His infamous use of impalement wasn't just a method of execution; it was a **deliberate tactic to instill terror** in his opponents. By impaling thousands of his enemies and displaying them along roads leading to his strongholds, Vlad created a psychological barrier that discouraged rebellion and foreign invasions.

The fear he generated allowed him to maintain control over a territory constantly under threat from both internal factions and external powers like the Ottoman Empire.

Vlad's ability to **navigate complex alliances** was another example of his strategic thinking. In a region caught between the Ottoman Empire and the Kingdom of Hungary, Vlad had to be adept at shifting alliances to suit his needs. Early in his rule, he aligned himself with the Hungarian regent John Hunyadi, securing military support that enabled him to reclaim the Wallachian throne. However, once in power, Vlad was careful not to allow his foreign allies too much influence. He understood that **Wallachia's autonomy** depended on balancing these powerful neighbors against each other, using them to his advantage when necessary, but never allowing them to dictate his policies. This ability to play larger powers against one another allowed him to retain independence while still securing the support he needed when faced with direct threats.

Vlad also demonstrated a keen ability to **capitalize on timing and opportunity** in volatile situations. When the Ottomans grew complacent or overextended, he launched **surprise raids** across the Danube, striking when they were least prepared and inflicting heavy casualties. These raids were not only tactically effective, but they also created the perception that Vlad was a **formidable and unpredictable enemy**, making it difficult for his opponents to anticipate his next moves. His strategic use of surprise attacks showed his ability to read the situation and exploit moments of weakness to strengthen his position.

Lastly, Vlad's reign offers a lesson in the importance of **decisive action** in volatile situations. He understood that hesitation could be fatal in a landscape where enemies lurked at every turn. His approach to leadership was often ruthless, but it was also **calculated and swift**. Whether dealing with rebellious nobles, foreign invaders, or potential allies, Vlad's ability to make decisive and bold moves kept him one step ahead of his rivals. His actions were always geared toward **securing long-term stability** in a region that had been defined by constant upheaval and betrayal.

In sum, Vlad the Impaler's rise to power and his reign demonstrate the value of **strategic thinking in times of chaos**. His ability to **identify and exploit weaknesses, use fear to his advantage, balance alliances, and act decisively** allowed him to capitalize on the volatile situation in Wallachia and transform a fractured land into a more unified and controlled state. His leadership, though brutal, offers timeless lessons in how to seize and maintain power in the most difficult of circumstances.

Chapter 3: The Impaler's Justice

Justice, in the eyes of Vlad the Impaler, was not about fairness or mercy; it was about maintaining absolute order and control in a land where disloyalty and rebellion were constant threats. Vlad's rule was defined by his unyielding approach to punishment, where even the slightest hint of betrayal or crime was met with extreme retribution. His infamous use of impalement as a method of execution became the symbol of his reign, serving not only as a tool for dispensing justice but as a powerful instrument of fear that would keep both his enemies and subjects in line.

For Vlad, justice was not a concept rooted in compassion, but in the belief that **order could only be maintained through terror**. The chaotic state of Wallachia, with its treacherous nobles and external threats, required a leader who could impose harsh discipline to prevent the country from descending into further chaos. Vlad saw his brutal punishments as a necessary means to an end, ensuring that those who challenged his authority would be made an example of, often in the most public and terrifying ways possible.

This chapter delves into Vlad's system of justice, exploring how his merciless punishments became an integral part of his strategy to secure his rule. From the mass executions of disloyal boyars to the gruesome impalements of enemy soldiers, Vlad's brand of justice was both a response to the constant threat of insurrection and a calculated display of his power. It was a justice designed not only to punish but to control—to create an environment in which fear ruled above all, ensuring that rebellion would never take root in Wallachia.

The use of impalement and other brutal methods to instill fear

VLAD THE IMPALER'S reign is most famously remembered for his use of **impalement** as a method of punishment and control. While medieval rulers often employed harsh methods to maintain order, Vlad took this to an extreme, making impalement his signature form of execution. It was not merely a tool for disposing of enemies but a calculated tactic designed to **instill terror** in anyone who might consider defying his rule.

Impalement itself was a particularly gruesome and slow death. Victims were pierced through the body with a sharpened stake, often inserted through the abdomen and emerging through the chest, mouth, or back. The stake was then planted in the ground, leaving the victim to die slowly over hours or even days. The sheer cruelty of this punishment was enough to spread fear across the land, and Vlad often ordered mass executions, leaving entire fields filled with impaled bodies as a **gruesome display of his power**.

One of the most infamous examples of this tactic was the so-called **"Forest of the Impaled,"** a horrific scene Vlad created to deter an Ottoman invasion. In 1462, as the Ottoman Sultan Mehmed II advanced into Wallachia, Vlad left behind a chilling welcome: **thousands of impaled corpses** lining the road to his capital, Târgoviște. Ottoman soldiers were so horrified by the sight that it weakened their morale and made them reconsider further incursions into Wallachia. This **psychological warfare** was as effective as any military strategy, as it projected an image of Vlad as a ruthless ruler who would stop at nothing to protect his territory.

Impalement was also used domestically to keep the **Wallachian nobility and commoners in check**. The boyars, who had been responsible for the betrayal and murder of Vlad's father and brother, were frequent targets of his wrath. Vlad would **impale entire groups of boyars** to eliminate disloyalty and send a clear message to others that rebellion would not be tolerated. In one notable incident, after inviting the boyars to a feast, Vlad had many of them impaled on the spot, while others were forced into grueling labor to build his fortress at Poenari. This act of **collective punishment** not only dealt with his immediate enemies but also solidified his reputation as a ruler who demanded absolute loyalty.

Impalement was not the only method Vlad used to maintain control. His reign was filled with stories of **horrific punishments** meant to instill fear and obedience. Thieves, adulterers, and traitors were often punished in the most extreme ways, including **boiling people alive**, **dismemberment**, and other forms of torture. These punishments were carried out publicly, ensuring that the message reached the entire population: any deviation from the laws Vlad imposed would be met with brutal consequences.

For Vlad, these methods were not merely acts of cruelty; they were part of a **larger strategy to maintain order** in a region plagued by instability. The chaos of Wallachia, with its frequent revolts and constant threat from foreign powers, required a ruler who could enforce strict discipline. Vlad believed that the only way to ensure loyalty was through the **fear of severe punishment**, and by making his punishments as visible and memorable as possible, he created an atmosphere in which rebellion was virtually unthinkable.

In using these brutal methods, Vlad established a reign built on **absolute fear**. His subjects and enemies alike knew that crossing him would lead to a fate worse than death, and in this way, he was able to maintain a grip on power in a land where treachery and betrayal had long been the norm.

Why Vlad believed that fear was essential to maintaining order and loyalty

VLAD THE IMPALER'S worldview was shaped by the harsh political realities of his time—where betrayal was common, alliances were fleeting, and power was constantly threatened by both internal and external forces. For Vlad, maintaining control over Wallachia, a small and vulnerable principality caught between two powerful empires, required a leader who could inspire not just respect, but fear. In his eyes, **fear was the most effective tool** for ensuring obedience, preventing rebellion, and safeguarding his rule against the constant threat of treachery.

One of the primary reasons Vlad placed such emphasis on fear was his personal experience with betrayal. His father, Vlad II Dracul, and his elder brother Mircea were both betrayed by the boyars (Wallachian nobility), leading to their deaths. This personal history of betrayal instilled in Vlad a **deep mistrust of the noble class** and a conviction that loyalty could never be assumed, only forced. For Vlad, fear became the mechanism through which loyalty could be extracted, as no one would dare challenge a ruler whose punishments were so extreme that even the thought of defiance would invoke terror.

Vlad also believed that **harsh justice was necessary to prevent chaos**. Wallachia was a land plagued by instability, with nobles constantly vying for power and foreign enemies, particularly the Ottomans, exerting pressure on the principality. In such an environment, Vlad saw **mercy as weakness**, a sentiment that would only invite further rebellion. He viewed swift and brutal punishment as the only way to establish **clear boundaries of behavior** for both his subjects and his enemies. By making examples of those who defied him, he could enforce **strict discipline** and prevent the kind of internal disorder that had destabilized the region for generations.

The chaotic political environment in which Vlad operated also contributed to his reliance on fear. Wallachia was a fragile state, caught between the Ottoman Empire to the south and the Kingdom of Hungary to the north. With these two empires vying for control over the region, Wallachian rulers often found themselves in precarious positions, unable to fully rely on either foreign power for protection. Vlad understood that Wallachia needed to appear as strong and **unshakable** as possible to deter both internal rebellion and foreign invasion. He knew that a reputation for **brutality and uncompromising justice** would make potential enemies think twice before challenging him or his territory.

Fear also served as a means to **maintain control over the fragmented Wallachian nobility**. The boyars had traditionally wielded significant power and were often behind the overthrow of rulers they saw as weak or ineffective. Vlad's ruthless purge of disloyal nobles and his systematic use of impalement were not only acts of revenge for past betrayals but also a calculated way to ensure that no one would ever dare conspire against him. His philosophy was simple: if the consequences of rebellion were horrifying enough, no one would risk defying him.

Beyond the nobility, Vlad's subjects lived under the constant threat of foreign invasion, lawlessness, and instability. **Strict laws and brutal punishments** helped create a sense of order and stability in a society where such things were often in short supply. Vlad's justice, though harsh, was seen by some as **necessary to protect Wallachia from collapsing into chaos**. By instilling fear, Vlad was able to maintain a degree of unity and control over a population that might otherwise have been divided by competing loyalties.

Moreover, Vlad's use of fear was not limited to Wallachia; he extended it to his enemies, particularly the Ottomans. By using **psychological warfare** and showcasing his brutal methods—such as impaling thousands of Ottoman prisoners—Vlad sent a clear message that he was not a ruler to be trifled with. This not only helped deter invasions but also strengthened his standing among his people, as they saw him as a fierce protector of Wallachian independence.

In Vlad's view, **fear was the foundation of effective governance**. In a world where power was constantly under threat and loyalty was never guaranteed, he believed that fear was the only reliable way to ensure obedience and maintain order. Whether dealing with rebellious nobles, foreign invaders, or his own subjects, Vlad used fear as his primary tool to consolidate his rule, stabilize his kingdom, and protect Wallachia from being torn apart by external and internal forces.

The psychological impact of terror on both enemies and subjects

VLAD THE IMPALER'S rule was defined by more than just the physical brutality of his actions—it was the **psychological terror** that left a lasting impact on both his enemies and his subjects. For Vlad, fear was not just a tool for punishment but a weapon of **psychological warfare**, designed to control the minds of those who might oppose him and ensure absolute obedience. The terror he inflicted was calculated to strike fear deep into the hearts of both external enemies and his own people, creating an atmosphere where the mere thought of defiance was enough to quell rebellion.

The **psychological impact on his enemies** was profound. Vlad's use of mass impalement and other horrific punishments sent shockwaves through the region. His gruesome tactics were meant to inspire dread and make his enemies hesitant to confront him. One of the most infamous examples of this was the **Forest of the Impaled**, where Vlad ordered the impalement of thousands of Ottoman soldiers and left their corpses on display for an advancing Ottoman army to see. The sight of their comrades' bodies impaled on stakes not only shocked the Ottoman forces but also weakened their morale. The message was clear: those who dared invade Wallachia would face a fate worse than death. This **psychological warfare** was as effective as any military strategy, as it instilled doubt and fear in the hearts of even the most seasoned soldiers, making them think twice before continuing their campaign against him.

For Vlad, this display of terror was a means of creating an **aura of invincibility**. By instilling fear before battle, he could reduce the resolve of his enemies, making them easier to defeat or, better yet, causing them to abandon their plans altogether. His reputation as a ruler who showed no mercy preceded him, and it became his most effective weapon in deterring invasion. Enemies knew that crossing Vlad meant facing **unimaginable horrors**, and this fear often accomplished what armies could not: it kept his adversaries at bay.

The **psychological toll on his subjects** was equally significant. Within Wallachia, Vlad's methods ensured that rebellion or disobedience was nearly unthinkable. The threat of impalement, or other extreme forms of punishment, hung over every action. Whether they were noble boyars or common villagers, the people of Wallachia lived under the constant fear that any deviation from Vlad's strict rules could result in a gruesome and public execution. This **constant fear of punishment** created an environment where Vlad's authority was unquestioned. Even those who might have been inclined to rebel knew that the consequences of failure were too horrifying to risk.

Vlad's approach to justice also ensured that **order was maintained** through fear. His reputation for brutally punishing thieves, corrupt officials, and anyone who broke his laws meant that crime rates were kept low. The people may not have respected Vlad out of love, but they **obeyed him out of fear**. His terror-induced rule created a sense of **stability**, where citizens knew that strict law and order were enforced, and any transgressions would be met with swift and merciless retribution. In this way, Vlad's reign, while brutal, brought about a level of control that had been lacking in Wallachia, where previous rulers struggled to maintain power.

The psychological impact of Vlad's rule also extended beyond the borders of Wallachia. His **infamous reputation** spread throughout Europe, where stories of his cruelty were circulated in the form of pamphlets and legends. These tales painted him as a monstrous figure, inspiring fear not only in his immediate neighbors but across the continent. Even in foreign lands, the thought of Vlad the Impaler evoked terror, ensuring that his reputation as a ruthless and invincible ruler endured long after his reign.

Ultimately, Vlad's use of terror was about more than just physical punishment—it was about **dominating the minds** of his enemies and subjects alike. By fostering an atmosphere of constant fear, he was able to maintain control over a volatile region and deter foreign threats. The psychological weight of his actions made people think twice before challenging his authority, ensuring that his rule remained secure. In Vlad's world, the fear of what could happen was often more powerful than any act of violence itself, and it was this **mastery of psychological warfare** that solidified his place in history as one of the most feared leaders of his time.

Chapter 4: The Politics of Brutality

For Vlad the Impaler, brutality was not just a tool of governance; it was a **political strategy**. In a region where power was constantly shifting and alliances were fragile, Vlad understood that fear alone could cement his rule in ways diplomacy and negotiation could not. His use of extreme violence wasn't arbitrary or the result of unchecked cruelty—it was a **calculated form of political maneuvering** designed to eliminate threats, secure loyalty, and project strength. Every act of brutality served a purpose, whether to crush internal dissent, intimidate rivals, or send a powerful message to foreign adversaries. In Vlad's view, a show of overwhelming force was often more effective than any negotiation or treaty.

In a volatile environment like 15th-century Wallachia, where betrayal was commonplace and external enemies were ever-present, Vlad's brutality served as a deterrent not only to local rivals but also to foreign powers like the Ottoman Empire and the Kingdom of Hungary. His actions, though extreme, were always deliberate, aimed at **controlling the narrative of power** and asserting dominance over those who might seek to challenge him. Vlad understood that the political landscape was as much about perception as it was about action. By creating an image of himself as an unyielding and ruthless ruler, he could discourage rebellion before it even began.

Vlad's use of **public executions and mass impalements** wasn't just to punish disloyalty; it was to send a message to all who might think of defying him. These brutal acts became a form of political theater—dramatic spectacles that demonstrated his unflinching commitment to maintaining order and his willingness to destroy anyone who stood in his way. He used these displays not only to deal with internal enemies, such as the disloyal boyars who had betrayed his family, but also as a **signal to foreign rulers**. The infamous "Forest of the Impaled" that greeted the Ottoman forces in 1462 was a deliberate act of psychological warfare, designed to sap the morale of his enemies and discourage further incursions into his territory.

But Vlad's politics of brutality were also aimed at creating a sense of **stability and control** in a land that had known little of either. Wallachia had long been a battleground for competing noble families, each vying for influence and power, often allying themselves with foreign interests. By eliminating his rivals through ruthless tactics, Vlad sought to unify Wallachia under his singular rule, creating a central authority that could withstand both internal treachery and external aggression. His acts of cruelty were, in this sense, a way of consolidating power and building the foundations for a more centralized state.

Moreover, Vlad's brutal approach wasn't confined to just crushing rebellion or repelling foreign invaders. He also used it to **impose a strict legal and moral code**. Under his rule, crime was virtually nonexistent, largely due to the **harsh punishments** meted out to thieves, corrupt officials, and others who broke his laws. Vlad saw law and order as key to maintaining stability in his principality, and his reliance on terror as a means of justice ensured that crime and disorder were dealt with swiftly and severely. This approach, while brutal, brought a degree of **peace and security** to a region otherwise plagued by lawlessness.

In the broader context of European politics, Vlad's brutality also had a diplomatic dimension. While many rulers viewed him as barbaric, they also recognized that his methods worked. His ability to repel the Ottomans and maintain a stable reign in such a turbulent region earned him a certain level of **begrudging respect** from his neighbors. They may not have approved of his methods, but they could not deny the effectiveness of his rule in keeping Wallachia from falling into chaos. In this way, Vlad's brutality was not only a tool for maintaining power but also for ensuring **Wallachia's independence** in a time of constant external pressure.

Ultimately, Vlad's politics of brutality were about **survival**. In a world where political instability and foreign threats were ever-present, Vlad understood that to maintain his power and protect his land, he had to use every tool at his disposal, including terror. He mastered the art of balancing fear with authority, ensuring that both his enemies and his subjects knew the price of defying him. This chapter will explore how Vlad's calculated use of brutality became the cornerstone of his political strategy, allowing him to navigate the treacherous waters of medieval Wallachia and secure his legacy as one of history's most formidable rulers.

Vlad's diplomatic relations with neighboring powers and how his reputation helped in negotiations

WHILE VLAD THE IMPALER is most famously remembered for his ruthless methods, his reputation as a **formidable and fearsome leader** also played a critical role in his diplomatic relations with neighboring powers. In a region fraught with instability and surrounded by larger empires like the **Ottoman Empire** and the **Kingdom of Hungary**, Vlad had to master the art of diplomacy just as much as the art of war. His brutality, while extreme, was a deliberate part of his political strategy that helped him navigate complex alliances, deter foreign aggression, and position Wallachia as a force to be reckoned with, despite its relatively small size.

Vlad's reputation for cruelty, particularly toward his enemies, was well-known far beyond Wallachia's borders. His infamous methods of punishment, especially impalement, were not just about local control—they became a powerful **diplomatic tool**. His enemies knew that crossing Vlad would result in horrifying consequences, and this knowledge often acted as a deterrent, allowing him to negotiate from a position of strength. For neighboring rulers and envoys, entering into negotiations with Vlad meant facing a ruler who was not bound by the traditional limits of mercy or diplomacy. His willingness to use extreme measures made his threats credible, and this gave him leverage when dealing with more powerful states like the Ottomans or the Hungarians.

In his dealings with the **Ottoman Empire**, Vlad walked a fine line between diplomacy and defiance. As Wallachia was positioned on the frontier of the Ottoman Empire, previous rulers, including Vlad's father, had been forced to pay tribute to the sultan as a means of securing peace. However, once in power, Vlad refused to remain a mere vassal. Initially, he paid tribute to the Ottomans to avoid immediate conflict, but he soon stopped and began launching **raids into Ottoman territory**, an act of outright defiance. His aggressive stance sent a clear message that he was not a ruler to be subjugated easily. When diplomatic envoys came from the Ottoman court, Vlad treated them with calculated cruelty, at one point **impaling the Ottoman ambassadors** who refused to remove their turbans in his presence. This was not merely an act of disrespect—it was a symbolic assertion of his independence and a warning to the Ottomans about the consequences of treating Wallachia as a subordinate state.

Despite his defiance, Vlad knew when to **balance aggression with diplomacy**. He cultivated relationships with other Christian powers, particularly the **Kingdom of Hungary** under the regency of **John Hunyadi**. Recognizing that he needed strong allies to fend off Ottoman advances, Vlad aligned himself with Hungary, securing military support to bolster his defenses against the Turks. His alliance with Hungary was also strategic in that it provided him with a buffer between Wallachia and Ottoman-controlled territories. The **shared goal of resisting Ottoman expansion** united Wallachia and Hungary in a delicate but mutually beneficial relationship, despite the frequent tensions between Wallachian rulers and their Hungarian counterparts.

Vlad's brutal reputation was useful in these negotiations, particularly in positioning Wallachia as a **necessary ally** for Christian Europe. His success in repelling Ottoman forces, combined with his fearsome reputation, made him a figure of **admiration and fear** among European leaders, even if they disapproved of his methods. They saw Vlad as a ruler capable of holding the Ottoman Empire at bay, a vital function in a region where the Turks sought to expand further into Europe. His cruelty toward the Ottomans, therefore, had a broader diplomatic effect: it signaled to the rest of Europe that Wallachia, under Vlad's leadership, could serve as a bulwark against Islamic expansion.

Additionally, Vlad used his reputation to **intimidate** not only his enemies but also neighboring rulers who might have sought to exploit Wallachia's precarious position. His brutal methods made others reluctant to interfere in Wallachian affairs, fearing that any conflict with Vlad would lead to gruesome consequences. This allowed him to maintain a degree of **autonomy** that other small states in the region struggled to achieve. Even powerful rulers, such as the Hungarian king Matthias Corvinus, knew that negotiating with Vlad required caution, as his unpredictable nature and his willingness to resort to violence made him a dangerous adversary.

Vlad's reputation as a ruler who ruled through fear did more than just deter potential invaders; it **enhanced his credibility** at the negotiating table. His ruthless actions created a powerful narrative—he was a ruler who would go to any lengths to protect his kingdom and uphold his sovereignty. This image allowed him to negotiate not from a position of weakness, as might be expected from a smaller principality like Wallachia, but from a position of strength, where the cost of betrayal or aggression was too high for many to consider.

In essence, **Vlad's brutality became a diplomatic asset**. His extreme actions made his threats believable and his rule secure, allowing him to navigate the complex politics of the region. By cultivating a reputation that combined both **fear and strength**, Vlad managed to wield a disproportionate amount of influence for a ruler of such a small state, keeping both foreign powers and internal enemies at bay. This strategic use of fear in diplomacy helped him maintain a balance of power in Wallachia, ensuring that his reign would be both feared and respected in equal measure.

Lessons in projecting strength and wielding fear to manage alliances and enemies

VLAD THE IMPALER'S reign offers enduring lessons in how **projecting strength** and wielding fear can be powerful tools in both managing alliances and deterring enemies. His success was not just due to his physical ability to control his subjects through brutality, but in the way he **harnessed fear strategically** to create an image of invincibility. By mastering the psychological elements of power, Vlad was able to maintain a fragile balance of influence among stronger empires like the Ottoman Empire and the Kingdom of Hungary, while also keeping his internal rivals at bay.

One of the key lessons from Vlad's rule is the importance of **maintaining an image of unflinching strength**, even when faced with overwhelming odds. Vlad knew that to protect Wallachia—a small and often vulnerable principality—he needed to be seen as a ruler who would go to extreme lengths to protect his throne. His practice of public displays of brutality, such as mass impalements, sent a clear message to both allies and enemies: **crossing Vlad would result in severe consequences**. The sight of thousands of impaled bodies along the roads leading into his kingdom was not just a physical deterrent but a **psychological weapon** that made even the most powerful forces think twice before challenging him.

This strategy of projecting strength wasn't just aimed at external enemies like the Ottomans—it was also crucial in **managing alliances**. Vlad's alliances with powerful figures such as Hungary's John Hunyadi and later King Matthias Corvinus were secured not through diplomacy alone, but through Vlad's demonstrated ability to **instill fear in his enemies** and keep his land stable under his iron rule. His reputation for **ruthless efficiency** in handling both internal and external threats made him a valuable ally, even if his methods were seen as extreme. By creating a persona of strength, Vlad ensured that his allies saw him not as a weak or unreliable partner, but as someone who could **hold his own against larger forces** like the Ottoman Empire.

Another lesson from Vlad's rule is that **fear can be a powerful tool in maintaining control over internal factions**. Wallachia's boyars had a history of betraying their rulers, shifting alliances depending on who held the most power. Vlad understood that trust in such an environment was fleeting, and that **loyalty could not be guaranteed without the use of fear**. His systematic purging of the boyars, particularly his brutal punishments for disloyalty, ensured that his rule would not be undermined by internal rebellion. Those who witnessed the gruesome fates of disloyal nobles quickly realized that Vlad's threats were not empty, and this **created an atmosphere of obedience** where rebellion was no longer an option.

Vlad also demonstrated the importance of **timing and selective cruelty** in wielding fear effectively. While he was often merciless in his punishments, he also knew when to temper his brutality with strategic foresight. For example, he occasionally allowed certain enemies or rivals to live if he believed it would benefit him politically, knowing that sparing a life at the right time could cultivate alliances or prevent future challenges to his authority. In this sense, Vlad's rule teaches the value of **measured brutality**—while fear must be constant, excessive cruelty without purpose can lead to instability. Vlad mastered the art of knowing when to strike and when to hold back, using fear as a tool that was both **unpredictable and strategic**.

Vlad's success in projecting strength also came from his ability to **turn fear into a diplomatic tool**. He understood that fear could be as effective in negotiations as military power. His refusal to bow to Ottoman demands for tribute, and his subsequent raids into their territory, were bold acts of defiance that shocked his enemies and demonstrated his resolve. These actions elevated his standing in the eyes of European rulers, who saw Vlad as a **bulwark against the**

Ottoman advance. His **fearsome reputation** made him a key player in regional politics, and this leverage allowed him to **negotiate from a position of strength**, even when his forces were numerically inferior.

The psychological impact of **strategic fear** also extended to his external enemies. The infamous "Forest of the Impaled," where thousands of Ottoman soldiers were displayed on stakes, was not just an act of cruelty—it was a calculated move to **demoralize and intimidate** his enemies. Sultan Mehmed II, upon witnessing the display, is said to have been deeply disturbed by the sight, a reaction that likely affected his willingness to pursue further conflict with Vlad. By using fear to project strength, Vlad managed to keep stronger powers at bay and protect his kingdom from being overrun.

Ultimately, Vlad the Impaler's reign teaches that **strength, when combined with the calculated use of fear**, can be a powerful means of controlling both allies and enemies. He demonstrated that **fear is a currency** that can be used to negotiate from a position of power, prevent internal dissent, and deter foreign invasion. Vlad's ability to maintain a fragile balance of alliances while keeping his enemies at a distance shows that **strategic brutality**, when wielded carefully, can be a vital tool in securing long-term stability and survival in the most volatile of circumstances.

Case studies: Diplomatic encounters with the Ottoman Sultan and Hungarian King

VLAD THE IMPALER'S reign was marked by a series of significant diplomatic encounters with two of the most powerful rulers of his time: **Sultan Mehmed II of the Ottoman Empire** and **King Matthias Corvinus of Hungary**. These encounters reveal how Vlad leveraged his reputation for brutality and his strategic use of fear to negotiate from a position of strength, even though Wallachia was a small and often vulnerable principality. Both encounters highlight Vlad's ability to navigate complex political dynamics with larger powers, using his fearsome image and tactical cunning to secure his goals.

Diplomatic Encounter with Sultan Mehmed II

ONE OF THE MOST FAMOUS encounters between Vlad and the **Ottoman Sultan Mehmed II** occurred when Vlad refused to pay the **tribute** that Wallachian princes had long been obligated to send to the Ottoman Empire. This was a bold and dangerous move, as Mehmed II had recently conquered Constantinople in 1453 and was at the height of his power, seeking to extend Ottoman influence deeper into Europe. Wallachia, as a small border state, was expected to submit to Ottoman dominance, but Vlad had other plans.

Initially, Vlad feigned compliance with Ottoman demands. He sent emissaries to Mehmed II, pretending to continue the tradition of paying tribute. However, behind the scenes, Vlad was preparing to resist Ottoman control. His **psychological warfare tactics** began when he **impaled the Ottoman envoys** who had come to Wallachia to collect the tribute, claiming they disrespected him by refusing to remove their turbans in his presence. This deliberate act of cruelty was meant to send a clear message to the Sultan: Vlad would not be intimidated, and Wallachia was not a vassal state to be easily controlled.

This led to a more direct confrontation in 1462, when Mehmed II sent an army to invade Wallachia and punish Vlad for his defiance. In response, Vlad employed **guerrilla tactics** and psychological warfare, including his infamous **Night Attack** on the Ottoman camp. Vlad's forces infiltrated the Ottoman encampment under cover of darkness, killing thousands of soldiers and creating chaos. The most chilling aspect of this encounter, however, came afterward when the Sultan and his forces marched into Wallachia and were met with the sight of **thousands of impaled Ottoman soldiers** outside the capital, Târgoviște.

This grotesque display, often referred to as the **"Forest of the Impaled,"** had a profound psychological impact on Mehmed II and his army. The Sultan, known for his own ruthlessness, was reportedly horrified by the scale and brutality of Vlad's punishment. While the Ottomans eventually withdrew from Wallachia, unable to sustain their campaign in the face of Vlad's guerrilla tactics and harsh environment, this encounter revealed how Vlad used **fear and terror as a diplomatic tool**. Rather than capitulating to Ottoman demands, he projected an image of strength and defiance that forced even a powerful ruler like Mehmed II to reconsider the cost of further aggression against Wallachia.

Diplomatic Encounter with King Matthias Corvinus

WHILE VLAD'S RELATIONSHIP with the Ottoman Empire was marked by hostility and defiance, his dealings with **King Matthias Corvinus of Hungary** were more complex, involving a delicate balance of alliance and betrayal. As the ruler of a Christian kingdom, Matthias Corvinus was a natural ally for Vlad in his efforts to resist Ottoman expansion. However, the relationship between Wallachia and Hungary was fraught with tension, as Hungarian kings had long sought to exert influence over the smaller principality.

In the early years of his reign, Vlad sought Hungarian support in his fight against the Ottomans. He aligned himself with **John Hunyadi**, the regent of Hungary and a staunch opponent of Ottoman expansion. Hunyadi provided Vlad with military backing that helped him reclaim the Wallachian throne in 1456. This alliance was crucial in allowing Vlad to fortify his position in Wallachia and resist Ottoman demands.

However, the relationship with Hungary took a turn in 1462, when Vlad, after his **defiance of the Ottomans**, sought refuge in Hungary following Mehmed II's campaign against Wallachia. **King Matthias Corvinus**, who had succeeded Hunyadi, was initially expected to support Vlad in his resistance against the Turks. However, Matthias was under pressure from the Papacy and other European rulers to focus on securing Christian unity against the Ottomans, and Vlad's brutal tactics, particularly against Ottoman prisoners, made him a controversial figure in European politics.

Matthias, rather than providing refuge and support to Vlad, **imprisoned him** in Hungary for several years. This was a politically expedient move, as it allowed Matthias to distance himself from Vlad's brutality and present himself as a more moderate Christian ruler in the eyes of Western Europe. However, even in captivity, Vlad's **reputation worked in his favor**. Although imprisoned, he was treated with a certain level of respect, and his fearsome reputation endured, making him a valuable political pawn in Matthias's larger diplomatic strategy.

In 1475, Vlad was released from imprisonment and once again supported by Matthias Corvinus to retake the Wallachian throne, as the political landscape had shifted, and Hungary needed a strong ruler in Wallachia to counter Ottoman advances. This turn of events demonstrated how **Vlad's reputation for brutality made him both a liability and an asset** in European politics. Despite his earlier imprisonment, Matthias recognized that Vlad's fearsome image and military prowess made him the right choice to lead the fight against the Ottomans in Wallachia.

Through these encounters with the Ottoman Sultan and the Hungarian King, Vlad showed that **fear, reputation, and calculated brutality** could be used as powerful diplomatic tools. His willingness to defy even the most powerful rulers, combined with his strategic use of terror, allowed him to navigate the complex political landscape of his time, securing his rule and defending Wallachia from external threats. These case studies illustrate how **Vlad's ability to project strength and wield fear** enabled him to negotiate and survive in a world dominated by larger and more powerful forces.

Chapter 5: The Night Attack: Lessons in Asymmetric Warfare

Vlad the Impaler's reign was defined by his ability to turn his military disadvantages into strategic strengths. Nowhere is this more evident than in his famous **Night Attack** of 1462, one of the most significant battles in his campaign against the Ottoman Empire. Outnumbered and facing the formidable forces of Sultan Mehmed II, Vlad knew that a traditional battle would likely lead to defeat. Instead, he resorted to **asymmetric warfare**, using unconventional tactics to strike at the heart of the Ottoman army in a surprise attack under the cover of darkness.

The Night Attack was not just a military maneuver; it was a lesson in how a smaller, less equipped force could use **surprise, terrain, and psychological warfare** to achieve victory against a more powerful enemy. Rather than confront the Ottomans head-on, Vlad employed guerrilla tactics, targeting their camp and sowing chaos among their ranks. His use of the element of surprise, along with the sheer brutality of his assault, crippled the morale of Mehmed's army and forced the Sultan to reconsider his campaign in Wallachia.

This chapter delves into the strategic brilliance behind Vlad's Night Attack and explores the lessons in **asymmetric warfare** that can still be applied today. From using the terrain to his advantage, to exploiting the weaknesses of a larger force, Vlad's approach demonstrated that a smaller, agile army could outmaneuver and destabilize a far stronger opponent. His mastery of these tactics not only saved Wallachia from

Ottoman conquest but also cemented his legacy as one of history's most cunning military leaders.

Vlad's most famous military tactics, including the Night Attack against the Ottomans

VLAD THE IMPALER'S reputation as a military leader was built on his ability to **adapt to his environment** and employ tactics that allowed him to counteract the overwhelming numerical superiority of his enemies. His methods were unconventional and brutal, designed not only to **inflict maximum damage** but to **demoralize** his opponents and create confusion in their ranks. One of the most famous examples of his strategic genius was the **Night Attack** against the Ottoman army in 1462, which remains a classic case of **asymmetric warfare**.

The Night Attack of 1462

IN 1462, THE OTTOMAN Sultan Mehmed II, flush from his victory in the conquest of Constantinople, turned his attention to Wallachia. With an army reportedly numbering **over 90,000,** Mehmed's force dwarfed Vlad's much smaller army of around **20,000-30,000** men. Rather than face the Ottomans in a traditional open-field battle, Vlad relied on **guerrilla warfare tactics**, using the terrain of Wallachia—dense forests, swamps, and mountain passes—to his advantage. He recognized that a prolonged siege or head-on engagement would favor the Ottomans, so he sought to wear them down through **hit-and-run attacks**, ambushes, and psychological warfare.

The **Night Attack** took place as Mehmed's forces encamped near the capital of Târgoviște. Under the cover of darkness, Vlad led a **raid deep into the Ottoman camp**, his men disguised as Ottoman soldiers to create confusion and fear among the enemy ranks. The primary objective was to **kill the Sultan** and disorganize the Ottoman forces. Although the attack failed to kill Mehmed, it caused chaos within the camp, with Ottoman soldiers mistakenly attacking each other in the darkness. The psychological impact of the assault was immense—by attacking at night and under such brutal conditions, Vlad instilled a sense of **fear and vulnerability** in his enemies, undermining their confidence in their ability to overpower Wallachia.

This strategy of exploiting **confusion and fear** allowed Vlad to achieve more than just a tactical victory. He demonstrated that even a much smaller force, if properly commanded, could cause significant damage to a larger, better-equipped enemy. The attack forced Mehmed to reconsider his campaign, and although the Ottoman forces eventually advanced, they did so under **diminished morale** and with increased wariness of Vlad's unpredictable tactics.

Guerrilla Warfare and Psychological Tactics

BEYOND THE NIGHT ATTACK, Vlad employed **guerrilla warfare** throughout his campaigns against the Ottomans. He was known for launching **lightning raids** on Ottoman supply lines, ambushing smaller units, and using the element of surprise to gain the upper hand. Vlad's forces would strike swiftly, inflict damage, and then **disappear into the wilderness**, leaving Ottoman forces disoriented and unable to mount an effective counterattack. These tactics reflected Vlad's understanding that **mobility and surprise** could neutralize the Ottomans' numerical and logistical advantages.

In addition to his military prowess, Vlad made full use of **psychological warfare**. He leveraged his reputation for cruelty to intimidate his enemies long before they even engaged in battle. The most infamous example of this was the **"Forest of the Impaled,"** where thousands of Ottoman prisoners were impaled on stakes and displayed outside Târgoviște for the advancing Ottoman army to see. This grotesque display served not only as a warning to the Ottomans but as a psychological blow that **sapped the morale** of Mehmed's forces. The fear of facing Vlad's brutal punishments spread throughout the ranks, making the prospect of further invasion less appealing.

Use of Terrain and Defensive Warfare

VLAD ALSO DEMONSTRATED an exceptional understanding of how to use **terrain** to his advantage. Wallachia's rugged landscape, full of forests, mountains, and marshes, provided ideal conditions for **defensive warfare**. Vlad's troops would lead the Ottomans deep into **narrow passes** and **ambush points**, where the large Ottoman army would find it difficult to maneuver. In many cases, **environmental factors**, such as harsh weather and difficult terrain, played a critical role in **weakening the enemy** even before direct confrontation occurred.

Additionally, Vlad made strategic use of **scorched earth tactics**. As the Ottomans advanced deeper into Wallachia, Vlad ordered the destruction of **crops, livestock, and villages** along their path, depriving the Ottoman army of supplies and forcing them to rely on overstretched supply lines. By the time they reached Târgoviște, the Ottoman forces were **weakened by hunger and disease**, making them even more vulnerable to Vlad's sudden and brutal raids.

Lessons from Vlad's Tactics

VLAD THE IMPALER'S military tactics highlight several enduring lessons in **asymmetric warfare**:

1. **Exploiting the Enemy's Weaknesses**: Vlad recognized that the Ottomans' size and reliance on traditional battle formations could be turned against them. By using surprise attacks, irregular forces, and harsh terrain, he exploited their weaknesses and minimized the advantages of their larger numbers.
2. **Psychological Warfare**: Fear can be as effective as force. Vlad's gruesome reputation and his brutal displays of

punishment undermined the morale of even the most formidable armies, sowing doubt and fear in their ranks before they even entered battle.

3. **Flexibility and Adaptation**: Vlad's tactics were not rigid. He adapted to the situation on the ground, switching between defensive and offensive strategies, using guerrilla tactics to achieve the most damage with the least risk to his own forces.

4. **Strategic Use of Terrain**: Vlad demonstrated how critical it is to know and use one's environment in warfare. By drawing the Ottomans into difficult terrain and exhausting them through scorched earth policies, he shifted the odds in his favor, despite their numerical superiority.

The **Night Attack** and Vlad's other military maneuvers proved that **asymmetric tactics** could be used to level the playing field against a much larger force. By leveraging his knowledge of the land, his fearsome reputation, and his understanding of psychological warfare, Vlad successfully defended his kingdom from one of the most powerful empires of the time, cementing his place in history as a master of **unconventional warfare**.

How to fight and win when outnumbered: lessons in guerrilla warfare

VLAD THE IMPALER'S success in resisting the much larger Ottoman Empire offers timeless lessons in **guerrilla warfare**—a form of combat that relies on **mobility, surprise, and psychological tactics** to offset the advantages of a larger, better-equipped enemy. Faced with overwhelming odds, Vlad understood that conventional warfare would lead to certain defeat. Instead, he turned to unconventional methods that focused on **striking at the enemy's weaknesses** rather than engaging in direct, large-scale battles. His strategies provide critical insights into how a smaller force can effectively take on a much larger opponent and even achieve victory.

1. Leverage the Element of Surprise

ONE OF THE FUNDAMENTAL principles of guerrilla warfare is the use of **surprise** to throw a larger enemy off balance. Vlad's **Night Attack** against the Ottomans in 1462 is a perfect example of this tactic in action. By attacking the enemy camp under cover of darkness, Vlad's forces were able to **sow confusion** among the Ottoman soldiers, many of whom mistakenly attacked each other in the chaos. The Ottomans, who expected a traditional battlefield encounter, were unprepared for this sudden, unpredictable strike.

The lesson here is that a smaller force can use **unexpected timing and unconventional approaches** to achieve significant results. Rather than engaging in a head-on confrontation, guerrilla forces should **strike when the enemy is least prepared**, catching them off guard and exploiting moments of vulnerability.

2. Use the Terrain to Your Advantage

VLAD'S DEEP KNOWLEDGE of Wallachia's landscape played a crucial role in his ability to **fight a larger force effectively**. The region's **dense forests, mountains, and swamps** provided natural defenses, which Vlad used to his advantage. He would lure Ottoman forces into **narrow mountain passes** or thick forests, where their numbers became a liability rather than an advantage. The larger Ottoman formations struggled to navigate the terrain, while Vlad's smaller, more mobile units could move quickly and strike decisively before retreating back into the cover of the wilderness.

This tactic teaches the importance of **terrain in guerrilla warfare**. A smaller force should always aim to fight on **familiar and advantageous ground**, where the enemy's superior numbers are neutralized. By forcing the larger force to fight in areas that are difficult to navigate, the smaller force can retain mobility and strike at will, frustrating the enemy's attempts to organize a counterattack.

3. Disrupt Supply Lines

WHEN FIGHTING A LARGER, well-equipped enemy, **disrupting their supply lines** can be as important as engaging them in battle. Vlad recognized that the Ottomans' vast army required a steady flow of food, weapons, and reinforcements to maintain their campaign. Rather than focusing on direct engagement, Vlad's forces conducted **lightning raids on Ottoman supply caravans**, ambushing them and destroying crucial resources before they could reach the front lines.

By **targeting logistics and supply chains**, a smaller force can weaken a larger army over time. Without food and supplies, even the most powerful armies will falter. Guerrilla forces should focus on **hitting vulnerable, undefended targets** that are critical to the enemy's ability to sustain their campaign. These strikes can gradually degrade the enemy's capacity to fight without requiring a major battle.

4. Hit and Run Tactics

VLAD MASTERED THE ART of **hit-and-run tactics**, which are essential in guerrilla warfare. His forces would launch **swift, surprise attacks** on Ottoman forces, inflict damage, and then retreat before the enemy could organize a counterattack. This strategy allowed Vlad to avoid prolonged engagements that would have been disastrous for his smaller army while still inflicting significant casualties on his opponents.

The key to effective **hit-and-run tactics** is **mobility and unpredictability**. A smaller force must be able to strike quickly and then vanish before the enemy can react. These attacks should focus on **soft targets**, such as supply lines, rear units, or smaller contingents of the enemy army, where a surprise attack can cause confusion and demoralization. By keeping the enemy constantly off balance, the smaller force can create the impression of being omnipresent and uncontainable.

5. Psychological Warfare

GUERRILLA WARFARE IS as much about **psychology** as it is about physical combat. Vlad understood the power of **fear** and used it to his advantage, employing **psychological warfare** to undermine the morale of his enemies. His tactic of **impaling thousands of prisoners** and leaving their bodies on display sent a chilling message to the Ottoman forces and their commanders. This grotesque spectacle not only demonstrated his ruthlessness but also planted doubt and fear in the minds of his enemies, making them question their ability to defeat such a merciless adversary.

In guerrilla warfare, the **psychological impact** of actions can be as important as their physical effect. Fear, confusion, and uncertainty can weaken an enemy's resolve, making them more cautious and less aggressive. A smaller force should seek to create **an aura of unpredictability and danger**, making the enemy constantly fear ambushes and sudden attacks. This psychological pressure can wear down a larger force over time, even if they remain physically superior.

6. Scorched Earth Tactics

ANOTHER LESSON FROM Vlad's approach to guerrilla warfare is the use of **scorched earth tactics** to deprive the enemy of resources. As the Ottomans advanced deeper into Wallachia, Vlad ordered the destruction of **villages, crops, and livestock**, leaving nothing for the enemy to use. This forced the Ottoman army to rely on its overstretched supply lines, which were already being targeted by Vlad's raids.

Scorched earth tactics can be devastating for a larger army that is dependent on local resources for sustenance. By **denying the enemy food, shelter, and supplies**, a smaller force can weaken their ability to maintain a prolonged campaign, creating conditions where the larger force becomes vulnerable due to hunger, exhaustion, and disease. This approach also buys time for the smaller force to regroup and plan further attacks while the enemy struggles to survive in hostile territory.

7. Exploit the Enemy's Overconfidence

ONE OF THE KEY ADVANTAGES a smaller force can exploit is the **overconfidence** of a larger opponent. The Ottomans, accustomed to overwhelming their enemies with sheer numbers, likely believed that Wallachia would be an easy conquest. Vlad played on this assumption by allowing the Ottomans to advance deeper into Wallachian territory, where his **hit-and-run tactics** and scorched earth policies gradually weakened them.

In guerrilla warfare, allowing the enemy to become **overextended and overconfident** can create opportunities for devastating counterattacks. A larger force may become complacent, believing that their numerical superiority guarantees victory, making them more vulnerable to **ambushes and psychological warfare**. By exploiting this arrogance, a smaller force can turn the tide in its favor.

Conclusion

VLAD THE IMPALER'S **asymmetric warfare tactics** offer valuable lessons in how a smaller, outnumbered force can take on and defeat a larger enemy. Through the strategic use of **surprise, mobility, terrain, and psychological warfare**, Vlad demonstrated that victory is possible even in the face of overwhelming odds. His ability to **disrupt supply lines, exploit the enemy's weaknesses, and instill fear** in his opponents allowed him to repel the might of the Ottoman Empire and maintain control over Wallachia. These principles remain relevant in modern guerrilla warfare, where adaptability and unconventional tactics often prove to be the key to victory.

How fear plays a role in psychological warfare

FEAR IS ONE OF THE most potent weapons in **psychological warfare**, and Vlad the Impaler understood this better than most. Throughout his reign, Vlad used **fear** not just as a method of punishment, but as a deliberate tool to manipulate his enemies and control his subjects. In the context of warfare, fear can be a far more effective weapon than physical force, as it influences the **mindset and morale** of the enemy long before they step onto the battlefield. By cultivating a reputation for **brutality and ruthlessness**, Vlad was able to weaken his enemies psychologically, often rendering them **incapable of fully committing to the fight.**

1. Paralyzing the Enemy with Fear

FEAR IS A POWERFUL emotion that can **paralyze decision-making** and hinder an enemy's ability to act. Vlad's reputation for extreme cruelty, such as his notorious use of **impalement**, played a critical role in his ability to instill terror in his adversaries. His enemies knew that capture meant more than just defeat—it meant facing one of the most horrifying deaths imaginable. This prospect often caused enemy forces to **hesitate** or **falter** in their plans to confront him, as the fear of what might happen if they lost became a significant factor in their decision-making.

For example, the **Forest of the Impaled**, where Vlad left thousands of Ottoman soldiers impaled outside the capital of Târgoviște, created such a profound sense of dread that even the highly disciplined Ottoman army was shocked. The psychological impact was immediate: the sight of such brutality sent a clear message that **fighting Vlad meant facing unimaginable suffering**, which lowered the morale of the invading forces and made them reconsider their willingness to continue the campaign.

This ability to **paralyze the enemy with fear** is a key aspect of psychological warfare. A leader who can instill fear can undermine the enemy's confidence and create an atmosphere of **anxiety and uncertainty**, where every action becomes clouded by the terror of potential consequences. Soldiers, already fatigued from battle, may find their **resolve weakened**, making them more prone to retreat, surrender, or poor decision-making.

2. Exploiting Reputation as a Weapon

VLAD'S REPUTATION FOR cruelty preceded him wherever he went. Even before engaging in battle, his **legend of brutality** spread across Europe and the Ottoman Empire, setting the stage for psychological warfare long before his army clashed with his enemies. Stories of his impalements, executions, and merciless tactics were widely circulated, enhancing the myth of Vlad the Impaler as a **ruthless and unstoppable ruler**. This reputation alone became a weapon, allowing Vlad to project **strength** and **invincibility** without having to fight as many battles.

Fear works on a **cognitive level**, where enemies build images in their minds of what might happen based on the reputation of their adversary. By cultivating this fearsome image, Vlad ensured that his enemies **feared him before even meeting him** in combat. Many opponents would be demoralized at the mere thought of facing him, leading them to underestimate their own abilities or overestimate the threat Vlad posed. This reputation-induced fear would cause hesitation, confusion, and ultimately defeat, as fear weakened the fighting spirit of his adversaries.

In modern terms, this is akin to using **propaganda or psychological operations (PSYOPs)** to spread fear and demoralize an opponent without engaging directly. Vlad's use of fear in this way illustrates how **reputation can be weaponized** to achieve strategic goals before a sword is ever drawn.

3. Fear as a Deterrent to Rebellion

VLAD DIDN'T ONLY USE fear against external enemies; he wielded it domestically to maintain control over his subjects and deter rebellion. In a region like Wallachia, where **noble families (boyars)** frequently challenged the ruler's authority, fear was an essential part of his strategy to prevent insurrection. Vlad's brutal punishments for disloyalty and treachery, such as **impalements, public executions**, and other gruesome displays, served as a reminder to his subjects of what awaited them if they dared to rebel.

This form of psychological warfare ensured that **loyalty was maintained through fear** rather than trust. Vlad's subjects lived in a state of constant fear, knowing that any betrayal, however minor, could result in the most horrific of punishments. By making an example of those who dared to oppose him, Vlad **discouraged rebellion** and ensured that his authority remained uncontested. In this way, fear acted as a **stabilizing force**, keeping potential rivals in check and preventing the formation of opposition movements.

4. Breaking Enemy Morale

IN WARFARE, MORALE is as important as military strength. An army with high morale can often fight through adversity and achieve victory even when outnumbered. Conversely, an army with low morale is vulnerable, and fear is one of the quickest ways to **erode morale**. Vlad understood that if he could **demoralize his enemies** before battle, he stood a much better chance of victory.

By employing **hit-and-run tactics, ambushes**, and his infamous **scorched earth policies**, Vlad created an environment in which his enemies felt **constantly under threat**. His guerrilla tactics caused Ottoman forces to feel as though they were being hunted, unsure of when or where Vlad would strike next. This constant state of anxiety, coupled with the fear of his brutal punishments if captured, led to **desperation and exhaustion** among Ottoman forces. When soldiers are constantly under stress and fear for their lives, they are more likely to make mistakes, flee, or abandon their objectives.

This strategy can be seen in the modern concept of **psychological attrition**—wearing down the enemy's will to fight through fear and anxiety rather than through direct military confrontation. Vlad's tactics demonstrate how **psychological warfare**, when executed effectively, can break an opponent's will to fight and lead to victory even when faced with superior forces.

5. Using Fear to Shape the Battlefield

FEAR ALSO ALLOWED VLAD to **shape the battlefield** to his advantage. His enemies were not just fighting against his army; they were fighting against their own fears. By controlling the narrative through fear, Vlad was able to dictate the terms of engagement. His opponents, whether Ottoman or boyar, often acted more cautiously or made defensive decisions based on their fear of what might happen if they fell into his hands.

This is a key principle in psychological warfare: **controlling the enemy's behavior through fear**. When an enemy is afraid, they are less likely to take bold actions or risks. They become more predictable, and their movements more cautious, which allows the smaller or defending force to anticipate and manipulate their behavior. Vlad's use of fear made his enemies second-guess their own strategies, effectively turning their psychological state into a tactical weakness.

Conclusion

IN THE HANDS OF VLAD the Impaler, fear became a **weapon as powerful as any sword or spear**. Through calculated acts of brutality, a fearsome reputation, and psychological manipulation, Vlad was able to wield fear as a tool to **control both his enemies and his subjects**. His success in using fear to paralyze, demoralize, and manipulate the battlefield provides a stark lesson in the effectiveness of **psychological**

warfare. Vlad's ability to project terror and turn it into a strategic advantage ensured that his enemies often **lost the war in their minds before the battle even began**, and it remains a defining aspect of his enduring legacy as a master of fear.

Chapter 6: The Impaler's Fortifications

Vlad the Impaler's reign was not only defined by his brutal methods of control and warfare, but also by his keen understanding of the importance of **fortifications** in securing his power. While his fearsome reputation often deterred enemies from direct confrontation, Vlad knew that a strong defense was equally critical to maintaining his rule. In a region like Wallachia, bordered by powerful empires and plagued by internal strife, Vlad took great care in building and reinforcing strategic **fortresses** that would serve as both military strongholds and symbols of his dominance.

His fortifications, including the infamous **Poenari Castle**, were not just physical defenses; they represented **psychological and territorial control**. Vlad's castles and strongholds were often situated in **rugged, mountainous terrain**, making them nearly impregnable to larger invading forces like the Ottoman Empire. These fortifications allowed Vlad to create safe havens from which he could launch attacks, defend against invasions, and assert his authority over a fragmented and often rebellious nobility.

Fortifications were essential in the defense of Wallachia, a land surrounded by enemies—**Hungary to the north**, the **Ottomans to the south**, and **internal factions** vying for control within. Unlike vast empires with expansive borders, Wallachia was a smaller principality, and its survival depended on **strategic defensive strongholds** that could withstand sieges and buy Vlad time to strike back against invaders. His fortresses, particularly Poenari Castle, were chosen and built with **military precision**, leveraging the natural topography of the

Carpathian Mountains to create defensive strongholds that were nearly impossible to penetrate.

Poenari Castle: The Heart of Vlad's Defense

ONE OF VLAD'S MOST important fortifications was **Poenari Castle**, perched high on a cliff overlooking the Argeş River. This castle, which became synonymous with Vlad's legacy, was both a refuge and a defensive outpost. Situated in an elevated, remote location, Poenari was nearly impregnable to attackers, who would have had to scale steep cliffs and navigate dense forests to reach its walls. Its location gave Vlad a **commanding view of the surrounding terrain**, allowing him to spot potential invaders long before they could approach. The castle was small but well-fortified, making it an ideal place for Vlad to retreat and regroup during times of conflict.

The construction and reinforcement of Poenari Castle itself is steeped in the legend of Vlad's brutality. According to some accounts, after executing many of the treacherous boyars who had betrayed his father, Vlad forced the survivors to **rebuild the castle** as punishment, compelling them to work under extreme conditions. Whether or not the stories are true, Poenari stands as a testament to Vlad's ability to **combine military strategy with psychological dominance**. By transforming the site into a fortress, Vlad ensured that it would become a powerful symbol of his authority.

Fortifications as Symbols of Power

FOR VLAD, HIS FORTRESSES were not only defensive structures but also **symbols of his strength and authority**. Each stronghold represented his ability to control the territory around it and to protect Wallachia from external and internal threats. They projected an image of **invulnerability**—a physical representation of his unyielding rule. Even in times of relative peace, the looming presence of these castles served as a reminder to his subjects and enemies alike that **Vlad was**

always prepared for conflict and that rebellion or invasion would be met with swift and decisive resistance.

Beyond Poenari, Vlad made use of **other fortresses and fortified towns**, enhancing existing defenses and building new ones where necessary. His strategic positioning of these fortifications ensured that Wallachia's key points of entry were protected, allowing him to **control access** to his kingdom. These strongholds served as bases from which Vlad could launch his guerrilla raids, retreat when necessary, and **safeguard his forces** during prolonged campaigns against the Ottomans or Hungarian nobles.

Use of Natural Defenses

A CRITICAL ASPECT OF Vlad's fortification strategy was his **mastery of the natural landscape**. Wallachia's rugged terrain, with its dense forests, high mountains, and winding rivers, became part of his defensive network. Vlad understood that a fortress's **location** was just as important as its architecture. By placing his fortifications in areas that were difficult to access, he made it nearly impossible for larger armies to deploy their full strength.

Vlad's use of **natural choke points**—narrow passes, river crossings, and mountain valleys—allowed him to control and funnel invading forces into areas where they were vulnerable to ambush. This combination of **natural and man-made defenses** turned Wallachia into a fortress state, where even the might of the Ottoman Empire struggled to advance. The terrain itself became a weapon, and Vlad's ability to integrate it into his fortification plans gave him a significant strategic advantage over his enemies.

The Strategic Purpose of Fortifications

WHILE THE DEFENSIVE strength of Vlad's fortifications is clear, their **strategic purpose** went beyond mere protection. These fortresses allowed Vlad to conduct his campaigns with **flexibility**. In times of invasion, he could retreat to his fortified strongholds, allowing his forces to regroup and plan counterattacks. His ability to retreat into fortified positions also made it difficult for his enemies to capture him or force a decisive battle. As a result, the **Ottoman army** and other invaders often found themselves bogged down in long, costly campaigns that drained their resources and morale.

The fortifications were also essential to Vlad's **psychological warfare** tactics. By retreating into his impregnable strongholds and launching raids from these positions, Vlad created an image of **invincibility**. His enemies may have outnumbered him, but they could never fully conquer him as long as he had a fortress to retreat to and regroup. This ability to endure made Vlad a formidable opponent and demoralized his enemies, who realized that even capturing territory did not guarantee victory.

Building strongholds and defenses to ensure power

VLAD THE IMPALER'S use of **strongholds and defensive structures** was a crucial element in his strategy to solidify and maintain power in Wallachia. In a region that was constantly under threat from both **external forces** like the Ottoman Empire and **internal factions** such as the boyars, Vlad understood that sheer military strength alone would not be enough to secure his reign. He needed to build a network of fortresses and defensive positions that would allow him to withstand sieges, repel invasions, and serve as symbols of his **unchallengeable authority**.

Fortifications as the Backbone of Power

VLAD'S DECISION TO construct and reinforce **fortifications** was driven by the volatile political and military environment in which he ruled. Wallachia, sandwiched between the powerful Ottoman Empire to the south and the Kingdom of Hungary to the north, was often caught in the crossfire of territorial ambitions. Beyond these external threats, the internal nobility, or boyars, frequently plotted against the ruling voivode. With **constant threats to his throne**, Vlad needed **strongholds** that could serve as **refuges** in times of danger and as **bases of power** from which he could project his rule over the region.

One of his primary fortresses was **Poenari Castle**, strategically located on a cliffside overlooking the Argeș River. This fortress was not only a military stronghold but also a symbolic representation of Vlad's reign. By choosing such an **isolated and nearly impregnable location**, Vlad ensured that he would have a **secure retreat** in the event of an invasion or internal revolt. Poenari's position atop steep cliffs made it difficult for even large armies to approach or besiege the fortress, giving Vlad a critical advantage over his enemies.

The Role of Fortifications in Repelling Invaders

VLAD'S STRATEGIC FORTIFICATIONS were designed not just to protect his own forces but to **frustrate and exhaust his enemies**. By building and reinforcing strongholds in **hard-to-reach locations**—often high in the mountains or deep in dense forests—Vlad forced invaders like the Ottomans to expend significant time and resources trying to capture these positions. This played into Vlad's broader strategy of **wearing down his enemies** through a combination of **hit-and-run tactics**, **ambushes**, and defensive warfare.

The **natural terrain** of Wallachia, full of narrow passes and treacherous landscapes, was a key element in Vlad's defense plans. By placing his fortresses in locations that were difficult to access, he made it almost impossible for large invading forces to deploy effectively. The combination of natural and man-made defenses allowed Vlad to **drag out campaigns**, creating a situation where invaders would be **isolated and vulnerable**. His forces could then launch raids from fortified positions, striking at the enemy and retreating to safety before a counterattack could be mounted.

Creating Psychological Barriers

VLAD'S FORTRESSES WERE more than just physical defenses; they were also part of his **psychological warfare strategy**. By constructing **strongholds** that appeared **impregnable**, Vlad reinforced his image as a ruler who could not be defeated. The sight of his **fortified castles** atop steep cliffs or hidden deep within the mountains served as a reminder to both his enemies and his subjects that Vlad's power was not easily shaken. His fortresses symbolized **stability** and **endurance**, projecting the idea that no matter how many times Wallachia was invaded or how many times his enemies tried to overthrow him, Vlad would always have a place to **retreat, regroup, and strike back**.

For his subjects, the presence of these fortifications sent a clear message: **rebellion was futile**. Even if Vlad's enemies managed to capture parts of Wallachia, his fortresses would remain unconquered. This made any resistance or revolt seem hopeless, reinforcing Vlad's dominance and discouraging challenges to his authority. His fortresses were not only practical defensive measures but also **psychological barriers** that made it difficult for opposition forces to envision a successful campaign against him.

Strategic Use of Fortresses in Military Campaigns

VLAD ALSO USED HIS **fortresses as staging grounds** for his military campaigns. In times of war, his fortified positions allowed him to maintain a **mobile defense**, where his forces could conduct **guerrilla raids** on larger invading armies and then retreat to safety behind fortified walls. The ability to move swiftly and then regroup in fortified positions allowed Vlad to **prolong battles**, causing his enemies to tire, lose morale, and eventually withdraw.

By utilizing **scorched earth tactics**—destroying villages, crops, and resources as he retreated—Vlad ensured that invading forces had little access to food and shelter as they approached his fortresses. This made it difficult for large armies, such as the Ottoman forces, to sustain prolonged campaigns in Wallachia. His fortresses, therefore, became critical points where he could control the **tempo and duration** of the conflict, forcing his enemies to fight on his terms and in locations where they were most vulnerable.

Fortifications as a Symbol of Rule

VLAD'S FORTIFICATIONS were not only defensive structures but also powerful **symbols of his reign**. The castles and strongholds he built and maintained became lasting reminders of his ability to **defend his territory** against all odds. They represented his **unwavering control** over Wallachia and his willingness to invest in the **long-term security** of his realm. Even after his death, these fortresses stood as enduring legacies of his rule, testaments to his understanding that

fortifications were as much about projecting power as they were about defense.

Vlad's strongholds helped to **secure his reign** by allowing him to maintain power in a region that was prone to both foreign invasions and internal strife. By constructing impregnable fortresses and placing them in strategic locations, Vlad ensured that his enemies would face insurmountable obstacles in their attempts to overthrow him. These fortifications, combined with his military tactics, created a **comprehensive defense network** that gave him a significant advantage over larger, more powerful forces.

Conclusion

BUILDING AND REINFORCING **strongholds and defenses** was a cornerstone of Vlad the Impaler's strategy to ensure his power in a highly volatile region. His **fortresses** not only provided physical protection but also acted as **psychological barriers**, deterring both internal revolts and external invasions. By strategically situating his strongholds in difficult-to-reach locations and integrating natural defenses into his plans, Vlad created a network of fortifications that allowed him to control the flow of battle and prolong campaigns, all while maintaining his authority over Wallachia. His legacy of fortification demonstrates that in times of conflict and instability, **defensive strength** can be as critical to maintaining power as offensive military might.

Insights into Vlad the Impaler's use of terrain and fortifications for control

VLAD THE IMPALER'S mastery of **terrain** and **fortifications** played a pivotal role in his ability to maintain control over Wallachia despite being surrounded by powerful and hostile forces. His understanding of how to use the natural landscape to his advantage, combined with his strategic placement of fortifications, allowed him to **dominate his enemies** and secure his rule. In an era where military strength alone was not enough to guarantee survival, Vlad used **the geography of his homeland** as a crucial element in his broader strategy of defense, control, and psychological warfare.

1. Exploiting the Natural Terrain for Defense

WALLACHIA, WITH ITS dense forests, rugged mountains, and winding rivers, offered a natural defensive advantage for a ruler who knew how to use it. Vlad recognized the importance of **geography** in defending his realm, and he strategically built fortifications in areas where the natural landscape could multiply their effectiveness. By placing castles and strongholds in **inaccessible locations**, such as the cliffs and mountain passes, Vlad ensured that his fortresses would be difficult to besiege or attack.

The natural **choke points** and **narrow passes** of Wallachia's mountainous regions were used to funnel invading forces into **vulnerable positions**, where they could be easily ambushed or delayed. By using the terrain to limit the movement of larger armies like the Ottomans, Vlad was able to turn the **numerical superiority** of his enemies into a disadvantage. This strategy forced his enemies to fight on his terms, in areas where their **mobility** and **size** were restricted, giving Vlad the ability to **strike swiftly** and retreat to safer ground before the enemy could fully respond.

2. Fortifications in Strategic Locations

VLAD'S FORTRESSES, such as **Poenari Castle**, were deliberately located in **strategic areas** that controlled important routes and entry points into Wallachia. Poenari, for instance, was perched on a high cliff, overlooking the Argeș River. This location allowed Vlad to monitor and control **river traffic** and movements through the region, making it a key defensive stronghold. The castle's elevation made it nearly impossible to breach, while its proximity to important routes ensured that Vlad could **control access** to his kingdom.

By constructing fortifications in such locations, Vlad created a **network of defensive strongholds** that gave him **control over key transit points** in Wallachia. These fortifications not only protected his territory from invasion but also allowed him to **regulate the movement of goods, people, and military forces** through his land. In this way, his fortresses became **both military and administrative tools**, reinforcing his control over the region.

3. Terrain as a Tool for Asymmetric Warfare

VLAD'S USE OF TERRAIN was closely tied to his **asymmetric warfare tactics**. Rather than meeting larger forces head-on in open battle, Vlad would use the terrain to **wear down and demoralize his enemies**. His guerrilla-style attacks were often launched from fortified positions deep in the mountains or forests, where his forces could remain **hidden and mobile**. The rugged landscape allowed him to launch **hit-and-run attacks** against larger Ottoman armies, forcing them to chase him through difficult and unfamiliar terrain.

This strategy not only allowed Vlad to **inflict damage on a much larger force** but also gave him the advantage of being able to **withdraw to fortified positions** that were difficult to assault. The psychological impact of having to fight in such hostile terrain, combined with the **fear of ambush**, often **demoralized invading forces** before they even engaged in battle. Vlad's use of terrain was thus an essential element of his ability to **prolong campaigns**, forcing invaders to spend valuable time and resources navigating difficult landscapes.

4. Psychological Impact of Inaccessible Fortresses

THE **remote and seemingly impregnable** nature of Vlad's fortifications added a **psychological dimension** to his use of terrain. His enemies knew that even if they managed to invade Wallachia, capturing Vlad or forcing a decisive battle would be nearly impossible as long as he had a fortress to retreat to. The inaccessibility of his strongholds, particularly Poenari Castle, made it clear that **Vlad could not easily be defeated**.

This psychological barrier worked in Vlad's favor, as it made his enemies reluctant to fully commit to campaigns against him, knowing that they could not easily overwhelm his fortifications. For his own people, the sight of these fortresses served as a reminder of **Vlad's strength and dominance**. They knew that their ruler was secure behind his defenses, which reinforced the **image of Vlad as an invincible leader** who could withstand even the most powerful external threats.

5. Scorched Earth Tactics and Terrain Control

IN ADDITION TO USING fortifications and natural terrain for defensive purposes, Vlad employed **scorched earth tactics** to deny his enemies the resources they needed to sustain prolonged campaigns in Wallachia. As his forces retreated into fortified positions, Vlad ordered the destruction of **villages, crops, and infrastructure**, leaving nothing for the invading forces to use.

By combining these tactics with the **difficult terrain**, Vlad ensured that the enemy would face severe logistical challenges. The **harsh landscape**, already difficult to traverse, became even more hostile without food, shelter, or support. The Ottomans and other invading forces were often left stranded in **inhospitable terrain**, their supply lines overstretched, and their morale deteriorating as they struggled to advance toward Vlad's fortresses.

6. Terrain and Political Control

BEYOND ITS MILITARY applications, Vlad used terrain and fortifications as part of his broader strategy for **political control**. By dominating the highlands and controlling access to strategic routes, Vlad could **manage the movement of his own nobility** and enforce his will over rebellious boyars. His fortresses were not just places of defense—they were **centers of power** from which he could impose his rule and maintain order within Wallachia.

The **geographic isolation** of his strongholds also ensured that **dissidents and rivals** had limited options for mounting rebellions or seeking external assistance. With the routes in and out of Wallachia firmly under his control, Vlad could prevent his enemies from **coordinating efforts against him** or seeking support from foreign powers like Hungary or the Ottomans. This strategic use of terrain allowed him to **centralize authority** in a region that had long been plagued by disunity and internal conflict.

Conclusion

VLAD THE IMPALER'S use of terrain and fortifications was a cornerstone of his ability to maintain control over Wallachia. By building strongholds in **strategic, inaccessible locations** and integrating natural defenses into his broader military strategy, Vlad turned the **geography of Wallachia** into a powerful tool for both **military defense and political control**. His fortifications not only protected his forces from invasion but also projected an image of **invincibility** that deterred enemies and discouraged rebellion. In the end, Vlad's mastery of terrain allowed him to resist powerful empires and maintain his grip on Wallachia, proving that **geography can be as critical to power as armies and weapons.**

How defensive measures contribute to long-term power and security

THROUGHOUT HISTORY, strong **defensive measures** have been critical in establishing and maintaining **long-term power and security** for rulers and nations alike. For leaders like Vlad the Impaler, who faced constant threats from both **external enemies** and **internal dissent**, building effective defenses was not only a means of protecting their immediate reign but also a key to ensuring the survival and stability of their territories over time. By creating **fortifications**, leveraging **natural terrain**, and employing **psychological tactics**, defensive measures can serve as powerful tools to consolidate authority, deter invaders, and secure a lasting legacy.

1. Protection from External Threats

THE MOST OBVIOUS ROLE of defensive measures is to protect against **external threats**—invasions, military campaigns, and sieges. For rulers like Vlad, whose domain of Wallachia was sandwiched between two powerful empires (the **Ottomans** and **Hungarians**), the ability to **defend key territories** was essential for maintaining sovereignty. Without strong defensive measures, any kingdom, no matter how large or small, risks being overrun by more powerful adversaries.

Vlad's construction of **fortifications** such as **Poenari Castle** was critical in creating **physical barriers** that protected his rule from invading forces. These fortresses, strategically located in hard-to-reach areas, made it difficult for enemies to quickly conquer or overrun Wallachia, allowing Vlad to defend his territory and resist the Ottomans despite their military superiority.

In the broader context, defensive measures like fortifications, city walls, and **garrisons** serve as **first lines of defense**, giving rulers time to regroup, launch counterattacks, or engage in diplomacy while under siege. When well-constructed and strategically placed, these defensive structures can discourage invasions altogether, as the cost of taking such fortresses often outweighs the benefits for potential attackers.

2. Internal Control and Deterring Rebellion

DEFENSIVE MEASURES also contribute significantly to **internal stability**. In regions plagued by disunity or where noble factions vie for power, a ruler must maintain **tight control** over key strategic locations to prevent rebellion or insurrection. Fortresses and defensive outposts allow rulers to keep watch over potential hotspots of dissent and to deploy troops quickly to areas where unrest may be brewing.

For Vlad, who faced **internal threats from the boyars** (the Wallachian nobility), his fortifications symbolized not only his military strength but also his **political control**. These strongholds served as **centers of power**, allowing Vlad to keep his rebellious nobles in check and ensuring that his rule extended across the region. By controlling access to key areas through fortifications and monitoring internal movement, Vlad made it nearly impossible for opposition forces to coordinate effectively or to seek assistance from outside powers.

Additionally, the presence of **impregnable fortresses** sends a clear message to potential rebels: **resistance is futile**. When fortifications are perceived as unassailable, the psychological impact on would-be challengers can discourage rebellion before it even begins. Knowing that a ruler has access to strong defensive measures often deters internal factions from attempting to seize power, helping to maintain **political order and long-term control**.

3. Psychological Impact and Deterrence

THE **psychological impact** of defensive measures plays a significant role in ensuring long-term power. Fortifications, when combined with an aura of **invincibility**, act as powerful deterrents, both for external enemies and internal challengers. The mere sight of a well-fortified castle or city can instill **fear and hesitation** in those considering an attack, making them question the feasibility of their plans.

Vlad's use of **psychological warfare**—which included placing fortresses in highly visible, strategically intimidating locations—added to his reputation as an **unconquerable leader**. His fortifications were more than just physical barriers; they were **symbols of his dominance** and control over the region. Enemies approaching his strongholds would already be demoralized by the knowledge that even if they could launch an attack, it would be a costly and potentially futile endeavor. This projection of **strength through defense** often deterred invasions and uprisings before they could gather momentum, contributing to the **longevity of his rule**.

This psychological factor is critical in warfare. By projecting **defensive strength**, rulers can **prevent conflict altogether**, reducing the need for constant military engagement and allowing them to focus on governance and long-term stability.

4. Time to Maneuver and Respond

ONE OF THE KEY ADVANTAGES of defensive measures is that they provide rulers with **time to maneuver and respond** in the face of crises. A well-fortified city or castle can withstand siege for weeks, months, or even years, giving the ruler time to **mobilize reinforcements**, engage in diplomatic negotiations, or wait out the enemy's resources. This ability to **delay conflict** and **outlast attackers** is a fundamental element of defensive strategy.

For Vlad, the ability to retreat to a **fortified position** like Poenari Castle allowed him to **regroup and reassess** his strategy during moments of crisis. It bought him valuable time to plan counterattacks, call for reinforcements, or even launch **guerrilla warfare** from a position of relative safety. The more time a ruler has to prepare and adapt to a situation, the greater their chance of maintaining power and turning the tide of battle.

5. Consolidation of Power and Territory

DEFENSIVE MEASURES are also critical for the **consolidation of power** over territory. By building and controlling fortifications in key areas, rulers can ensure that their authority extends across their realm. Fortresses serve not only as military bases but also as **administrative centers** from which local governance can be controlled. This enables rulers to **exercise authority** over distant or difficult-to-reach regions, ensuring that their rule remains unchallenged.

For Vlad, his network of fortifications allowed him to **project power across Wallachia**, even in remote areas where his presence might not have been felt otherwise. His fortresses acted as **symbols of his authority**, ensuring that both his subjects and external powers recognized the extent of his control. This **centralization of power** through defensive structures helped Vlad consolidate his hold on the region, allowing him to govern effectively even in times of unrest or invasion.

6. Longevity of Rule and Legacy

PERHAPS MOST IMPORTANTLY, defensive measures contribute to the **longevity of a ruler's reign** and create a lasting **legacy of stability**. A ruler who invests in fortifications and defensive infrastructure leaves behind not only a physical reminder of their reign but also a system that continues to protect and defend the region long after they are gone. These defensive structures become part of the **foundational security** of the territory, ensuring that future generations can benefit from the stability they provide.

Vlad's fortifications, particularly Poenari Castle, remain enduring symbols of his strategic brilliance and ability to **safeguard Wallachia** from external threats. Long after his death, these structures continued to protect the region, cementing his legacy as a ruler who understood that **defensive strength is the key to lasting power.** The **long-term security** provided by such fortifications ensured that Wallachia remained resistant to outside invasion, even in the turbulent periods that followed his reign.

Conclusion

VLAD THE IMPALER'S use of **defensive measures**—from well-placed fortifications to exploiting natural terrain—demonstrates how rulers can use **strong defenses to secure long-term power** and stability. By protecting against external threats, maintaining internal control, and leveraging the psychological impact of defensive strength, rulers can deter challenges and **consolidate their authority.** Effective defensive measures offer a ruler time to respond to crises, control their territory, and project an image of invincibility, ensuring that their reign is not only secure but that their legacy endures. Defensive measures, when properly implemented, become the foundation upon which **lasting power** is built.

Chapter 7: Dealing with Internal Rebellions

For rulers like Vlad the Impaler, maintaining control over a kingdom was not just about defending against foreign enemies—it was about ensuring **internal stability** in a region where rebellion and betrayal were constant threats. Throughout his reign, Vlad faced significant opposition from the **Wallachian nobility (boyars)**, who had a long history of plotting against their rulers, often switching allegiances depending on which faction held the most power. Internal rebellions were a serious danger, capable of undermining a ruler's authority, destabilizing the region, and inviting foreign intervention.

Vlad's response to these threats was swift and brutal. He viewed **rebellion** not just as disobedience but as a fundamental challenge to his **right to rule**. To secure his throne, he developed a series of **ruthless tactics** to suppress internal dissent and prevent future uprisings. His methods, though extreme, were highly effective in instilling **fear** and **obedience**, ensuring that any thoughts of rebellion were quashed before they could gain momentum.

This chapter explores Vlad's approach to handling internal rebellions, from his use of **public executions** and **mass impalements** to his strategic manipulation of noble factions. By employing fear as a tool and making an example of those who opposed him, Vlad created an atmosphere of **unwavering loyalty**—or at least **paralyzing fear**—within his realm, cementing his control over Wallachia.

The internal challenges Vlad faced from nobility and traitors

VLAD THE IMPALER'S rule was constantly under threat from within, particularly from the **Wallachian nobility, or boyars**, who held significant power and influence in the region. The boyars had a long history of **betraying their rulers**, often siding with foreign powers or rival factions whenever it suited their personal interests. This deeply entrenched system of noble control made it difficult for any voivode (prince) to maintain long-term stability, and Vlad's reign was no exception. His father, Vlad II Dracul, had been betrayed and killed by the boyars, and his brother, Mircea, was tortured and buried alive by these same nobles. This personal history of betrayal had a profound impact on Vlad's approach to governance, shaping his **ruthless methods** of dealing with internal dissent.

1. Nobility's Power and Influence

THE **boyars** were not only powerful landowners but also influential in Wallachian politics. They controlled vast estates and commanded loyalty from those who lived and worked on their lands. Over time, the boyars had grown accustomed to manipulating the throne, often choosing to support or overthrow voivodes based on their own interests. For centuries, this noble class played a critical role in the political instability of Wallachia, which saw frequent changes in leadership as boyar factions switched allegiances to advance their own power. The boyars, therefore, were not just subjects of the ruler; they were powerful **rival factions** who could easily become traitors if they believed their interests were threatened.

When Vlad III ascended to the throne, he faced this deeply entrenched system of **noble power**, where many of the boyars saw the ruler as a tool they could manipulate rather than an absolute authority to respect. For Vlad, this presented a direct challenge to his legitimacy and ability to rule effectively. He quickly realized that if he was to maintain control over Wallachia, he needed to break the boyars' power and prevent them from continuing their tradition of **treachery**.

2. Betrayal of His Father and Brother

VLAD'S HATRED OF THE boyars was deeply personal. In 1447, his father, Vlad II Dracul, was betrayed and killed by rebellious boyars who had aligned themselves with Hungary to remove him from power. His elder brother, Mircea, suffered an even more brutal fate—**tortured and buried alive** by the same boyars who sought to eliminate any potential claimants to the Wallachian throne. This traumatic loss solidified Vlad's belief that the nobility were **disloyal opportunists** who could never be trusted. His experiences with betrayal shaped his rule, driving him to pursue **revenge** and ensure that he would never face the same fate as his father and brother.

This personal vendetta against the boyars led Vlad to view any form of rebellion or disloyalty as a **threat to his survival**, which he would meet with extreme punishment. In his mind, rebellion was not just a political issue; it was a **matter of life and death**. If he did not eliminate the boyars' ability to challenge his authority, his rule would always be at risk, and his family's tragic fate could repeat itself.

3. Noble Factions and Foreign Influence

IN ADDITION TO THEIR internal power struggles, the boyars often sought to align themselves with **foreign powers** like the Ottoman Empire or the Kingdom of Hungary, which had their own designs on Wallachia. These alliances with outside forces further complicated Vlad's efforts to maintain control. The boyars would often **switch allegiances** depending on which foreign power offered them the best opportunity to advance their own interests, leaving Wallachia vulnerable to foreign intervention and exploitation.

Vlad's control over Wallachia was constantly challenged by these noble factions who sought to use his reign as a way to negotiate better terms for themselves with Hungary or the Ottomans. This complex web of **loyalties and betrayals** made ruling Wallachia a perilous endeavor. Vlad had to contend not only with the threat of rebellion from within but also with the possibility that his own nobles were conspiring with foreign enemies to undermine him. The fluid loyalties of the boyars made it impossible for Vlad to rule without constant vigilance, as even those who professed loyalty could be plotting against him in secret.

4. The First Rebellion and the Easter Feast

ONE OF THE MOST NOTABLE internal challenges Vlad faced from the nobility came early in his reign when he dealt decisively with the boyars who had conspired against his family. In an act of both **revenge** and **political calculation**, Vlad invited many of the boyars to an Easter feast in 1457, ostensibly to celebrate the holiday. However, the event quickly turned into a bloodbath. Vlad **seized the boyars**, accusing them of treachery and of being responsible for his father and brother's deaths. Many of the older nobles were **impaled on the spot**, while the younger ones were forced into hard labor, sent to the mountains to rebuild **Poenari Castle**, one of Vlad's key fortifications.

This brutal act of **mass execution and punishment** was designed not only to avenge his family but also to **break the power of the boyars** and send a clear message: rebellion would be met with extreme consequences. By publicly and violently eliminating those who had betrayed his father, Vlad demonstrated that his rule would be different—**disloyalty would not be tolerated**, and the nobility would no longer hold the same power over the throne.

5. Suppressing Future Rebellions

EVEN AFTER THIS INITIAL act of revenge, Vlad faced continued opposition from the nobility, many of whom resented his efforts to centralize power and weaken their influence. Throughout his reign, he used **brutal tactics** to suppress any sign of rebellion or dissent among the nobility. His **public executions, impalements**, and other gruesome punishments were not just acts of cruelty but deliberate efforts to **instill fear** in those who might consider challenging his rule.

Vlad's **reputation for cruelty** became a powerful deterrent, ensuring that any noble who contemplated rebellion would think twice about the consequences. His tactics were effective in **creating an atmosphere of fear**, where the consequences of betrayal were so severe that few were willing to take the risk. Vlad's ability to keep the nobility in check through fear allowed him to consolidate his power and maintain control over Wallachia for much of his reign.

Conclusion

THE **internal challenges** Vlad faced from the nobility and traitors were perhaps some of the greatest threats to his rule. The Wallachian boyars, with their history of betrayal and shifting loyalties, represented a constant danger that could undermine his authority at any moment. Vlad's response to these challenges was to use **brutality and fear** to eliminate the boyars' power, suppress rebellions, and secure his throne. His personal history of betrayal, combined with the political realities of ruling Wallachia, drove Vlad to adopt ruthless measures in dealing with internal dissent, ensuring that his reign would be defined by **absolute control** and **unyielding authority**.

How Vlad the Impaler managed disloyalty and rebellion through swift and brutal action

VLAD THE IMPALER'S rule over Wallachia was marked by a relentless and **ruthless approach** to dealing with disloyalty and rebellion. His personal experiences with betrayal, particularly the death of his father and brother at the hands of disloyal boyars, left him with an acute understanding that **power could only be maintained through decisive and brutal action**. Vlad's methods were extreme, but they were also effective in ensuring **obedience and loyalty**, creating an atmosphere of **fear** that kept both internal and external threats at bay.

Vlad's strategy for managing disloyalty and rebellion was based on the principle that **swift punishment** was the key to preventing further unrest. By acting quickly and publicly against those who opposed him, he created a **culture of terror** that made others think twice before challenging his authority. His use of **impalement**, public executions, and other forms of brutal punishment not only eliminated immediate threats but also served as a powerful deterrent against future acts of defiance. This chapter delves into the tactics Vlad used to deal with internal dissent, exploring how his **ruthless actions** helped him maintain control in a volatile political landscape.

1. Impalement as a Symbol of Power

PERHAPS THE MOST NOTORIOUS method Vlad used to deal with disloyalty was **impalement**, which became synonymous with his reign. Vlad used this particularly gruesome form of execution not only as punishment but as a way to **instill fear** in both his enemies and his subjects. Impalement was designed to be a slow, agonizing death, often carried out in public places where large numbers of people could witness the suffering of the condemned. This act was not just a method of eliminating his enemies but a form of **psychological warfare**, sending a clear message to anyone who might consider opposing him.

One of the most famous examples of Vlad's use of impalement came early in his reign when he dealt with the **treacherous boyars** who had conspired against his family. After inviting them to an Easter feast in 1457, Vlad **seized and impaled** the older boyars who had betrayed his father. This mass impalement was not only a swift response to disloyalty but a calculated act of **revenge** and a public demonstration of his absolute power. By making such an example of the boyars, Vlad ensured that future dissenters understood the consequences of treachery.

Impalement became a tool of **control and deterrence**. The fear of suffering such a horrifying fate prevented many would-be rebels from acting against Vlad, as they knew that disloyalty would be met with the most extreme punishment imaginable. This tactic was successful in discouraging rebellion, as the terror it instilled in the population made defiance seem not only dangerous but suicidal.

2. Decisive Elimination of Threats

VLAD UNDERSTOOD THAT **swift and decisive action** was necessary to maintain control in a land rife with political intrigue. He did not hesitate to eliminate perceived threats quickly and thoroughly. Rather than engaging in long, drawn-out trials or political negotiations, Vlad chose to **strike first** and with overwhelming force, ensuring that any opposition was crushed before it could gain momentum.

One of the key examples of this approach was his handling of **internal revolts** and **conspiracies**. When Vlad suspected nobles or officials of plotting against him, he acted without hesitation, often ordering their **immediate execution**. His use of public executions served a dual purpose: it removed potential threats while reinforcing his authority. Vlad knew that any sign of weakness would embolden his enemies, so his **merciless responses** to even minor acts of disloyalty created a reputation of invincibility and ensured that potential conspirators would be too afraid to act.

This principle of **eliminating threats swiftly** extended to his dealings with external enemies as well. Vlad did not wait for his enemies to strike first—he often launched **preemptive attacks** to neutralize them before they could pose a serious challenge to his rule. This approach demonstrated his **decisiveness as a leader**, making it clear that any challenge to his power would be met with immediate and brutal consequences.

3. Public Displays of Punishment

ONE OF VLAD'S MOST effective methods for managing disloyalty was his use of **public punishments**. By conducting executions in highly visible locations and in front of large audiences, Vlad ensured that his punishments were not just **retributive** but **instructive**. These public displays of brutality were designed to send a message to the entire population: **disobedience would not be tolerated**, and the cost of rebellion was death in the most horrifying form possible.

Vlad used public executions to **set an example**, demonstrating that no one—whether noble or commoner—was above his rule. For instance, in dealing with **corruption and theft**, Vlad was known to execute those caught stealing or embezzling in front of the local population, sometimes impaling them in the very town square where the crime had occurred. These **public spectacles** reinforced his image as a just but ruthless ruler, willing to punish any transgressor regardless of their social standing.

This use of public punishment was part of a larger strategy to **instill fear and respect**. By making an example of a few, Vlad could **control the many**. The sight of impaled bodies lining the roads or displayed outside city gates served as a constant reminder of the consequences of defying the voivode. This form of **psychological warfare** was essential in maintaining order and ensuring that even those who harbored rebellious thoughts would be too afraid to act on them.

4. Suppressing Noble Power

ONE OF VLAD'S MOST significant internal challenges came from the **boyars**, the powerful nobles who had historically played a central role in Wallachian politics. The boyars had a long history of **betraying and undermining** their rulers, and Vlad was determined to break their influence. His handling of the boyars was marked by swift and **brutal reprisals**, often involving mass executions or forced labor for those who were spared immediate death.

After his **Easter feast massacre**, where he impaled many of the older boyars, Vlad systematically worked to **dismantle the power** of the nobility. He replaced many of the disloyal nobles with men of **lower birth**, who were more loyal and dependent on him for their positions. This tactic not only removed immediate threats but also created a **new class of loyalists** who owed their status and survival to Vlad's favor.

By targeting the nobility with such decisive and brutal actions, Vlad was able to **neutralize their power** and prevent future rebellions. His reputation for ruthlessness ensured that the remaining nobles would be too afraid to plot against him, knowing that any attempt at rebellion would be met with swift and brutal retaliation.

5. Use of Fear as a Deterrent

FEAR WAS VLAD'S MOST powerful weapon in managing disloyalty and rebellion. His entire reign was built around the concept that **fear could control populations** more effectively than mercy or leniency. Vlad's **calculated acts of brutality** were designed not only to punish but to **deter** others from even considering rebellion. The fear of death by impalement or other gruesome punishments created a

psychological barrier that made it nearly impossible for internal conspiracies to gain traction.

This use of fear extended to both his enemies and his subjects. Vlad's reputation as a **ruthless and merciless ruler** preceded him, and even those who had never personally experienced his punishments knew of the consequences of defiance. By cultivating a fearsome image, Vlad created an environment where **loyalty was the only rational choice**. The effectiveness of this strategy is evident in the fact that few significant internal rebellions occurred after Vlad's initial brutal purges.

Conclusion

VLAD THE IMPALER'S approach to managing disloyalty and rebellion was defined by **swift and brutal action**, ensuring that any challenge to his authority was met with immediate and overwhelming force. Through the use of **public executions, impalements**, and decisive reprisals, Vlad instilled **fear** in both his subjects and enemies, creating an atmosphere where rebellion seemed not only futile but suicidal. His ability to **eliminate threats quickly** and use public punishments as a tool of **psychological warfare** allowed him to maintain control over Wallachia despite the constant challenges posed by internal factions and foreign powers. Vlad's reign stands as a stark example of how **fear, when wielded effectively**, can be a powerful tool in maintaining order and consolidating power.

The balance between fear and fairness in governance

VLAD THE IMPALER'S reign is often remembered for its **brutality and fear**, yet his rule also highlights an important aspect of governance: the balance between fear and fairness. While Vlad is infamous for his ruthless methods, his governance was not purely based on cruelty for cruelty's sake. He understood that fear was a powerful tool to maintain **control and deter rebellion**, but he also recognized the need for **fairness and justice** in order to sustain long-term stability and loyalty among his people.

Striking a balance between fear and fairness is crucial for any ruler, as **excessive brutality** can lead to resentment, while **over-leniency** can embolden disloyalty and rebellion. Vlad's reign demonstrates that fear alone cannot sustain a ruler's power indefinitely—there must also be a sense of **justice** that resonates with the governed. By addressing crime, corruption, and disloyalty with swift and decisive action, Vlad earned a reputation for **enforcing order**. At the same time, by applying **justice fairly** to all, regardless of social standing, he ensured that his people saw him as a **protector of law and order**, not just a tyrant.

1. Fear as a Tool for Stability

FEAR WAS THE CORNERSTONE of Vlad's governance strategy. His notorious use of **public executions, impalements**, and brutal punishments created a powerful deterrent against disloyalty and rebellion. By instilling fear, Vlad ensured that both his subjects and enemies were hesitant to act against him. Fear allowed him to maintain **stability in a land constantly threatened by internal power struggles** and foreign invasions.

For Vlad, fear was a tool to enforce **obedience** and prevent challenges to his rule. In the chaotic political landscape of Wallachia, where betrayal and shifting loyalties were commonplace, Vlad understood that a show of **brutal force** was necessary to command respect. His public displays of punishment served as a **warning** to all who might defy him, ensuring that rebellion seemed like a suicidal endeavor. The use of fear was not just a reaction to disloyalty—it was a **preemptive strategy** to deter disobedience and consolidate his power.

However, fear alone could not sustain a kingdom. Excessive use of brutality without a sense of justice would have risked alienating the very people Vlad sought to control. To avoid descending into sheer tyranny, he needed to temper fear with **fairness**.

2. Fairness as a Tool for Legitimacy

WHILE VLAD RULED THROUGH fear, he also understood the importance of **fairness and justice** to establish legitimacy and long-term stability. His reign was not simply characterized by unchecked cruelty but by a **strict enforcement of laws** that applied to both the nobility and the common people. In a region where lawlessness and corruption were rampant, Vlad positioned himself as a **defender of order**. His brutal punishments for crimes like **theft, corruption, and treachery** were often seen as harsh but **necessary** to restore peace and stability in Wallachia.

Vlad's application of justice was marked by a sense of **fairness** that resonated with his subjects, particularly those who had suffered under corrupt and disloyal nobles. By punishing corrupt officials and dishonest merchants, Vlad sought to **cleanse the land of injustice**. His strict laws ensured that even the powerful boyars could not escape punishment if they broke the law, which earned him the respect of common people who often viewed the nobility as untouchable.

Vlad's fairness was not about **leniency**; rather, it was about **applying the law equally**, regardless of social status. This sense of justice helped him maintain his authority, as the people of Wallachia could see that Vlad's harsh measures were aimed not just at instilling fear but at creating a more just and orderly society. By establishing a reputation as a **fair but ruthless ruler**, Vlad gained **legitimacy** in the eyes of many of his subjects, who came to see him as a **protector against the corrupt elite**.

3. Punishing the Guilty, Protecting the Innocent

VLAD'S APPROACH TO governance focused on the principle that **those who broke the law deserved punishment**, while those who remained loyal and law-abiding would be protected. This clear distinction between **right and wrong** allowed Vlad to balance his use of fear with a sense of **justice**. While his methods were undoubtedly severe, they were also seen as a way of maintaining **social order** in a time of chaos.

For example, Vlad's harsh punishments for **theft and dishonesty** were not acts of senseless cruelty but were intended to create a safer and more stable society. In a region where lawlessness was widespread, Vlad's ability to **enforce strict laws** provided a sense of security for ordinary people. His swift actions against criminals—whether noble or common—made it clear that his rule was **fair in its severity**. Those who followed the law had nothing to fear, but those who violated it would face the full extent of his brutal justice.

This approach helped Vlad maintain the loyalty of his people, even as he ruled through fear. The **innocent were protected**, while the guilty were punished, which gave his reign a sense of **moral clarity**. His reputation for **swift and impartial justice** made it clear that under his rule, no one was above the law—an important factor in maintaining long-term power.

4. Fear and Fairness as Complementary Forces

VLAD'S REIGN DEMONSTRATED that **fear and fairness** are not mutually exclusive but can be complementary forces in governance. Fear was necessary to deter disloyalty and prevent rebellion, while fairness provided the **legitimacy** and **moral authority** needed to govern effectively. By applying the law equally and without favoritism, Vlad created a sense of **justice** that balanced his harsh methods.

This balance was crucial for maintaining **long-term stability**. Without fairness, fear alone could lead to resentment, rebellion, and instability, as people would see the ruler as a tyrant who governed through cruelty for its own sake. Without fear, fairness alone might not have been enough to deter the constant threats posed by the boyars and foreign powers. By blending the two, Vlad ensured that his rule was **feared but also respected**—a combination that allowed him to maintain control over Wallachia in a time of great uncertainty.

Vlad's ability to balance fear and fairness helped create an atmosphere in which his subjects knew that while he ruled with an iron fist, his actions were **just and necessary** for the survival of the kingdom. This approach allowed him to **deter potential rebels** while maintaining **legitimacy in the eyes of his people**.

5. The Risks of Excessive Fear

WHILE FEAR WAS A POWERFUL tool for Vlad, it also posed certain risks if overused. Excessive brutality without a clear sense of justice could lead to **alienation and unrest**. If people began to see fear as the only driving force of governance, the ruler risked losing their loyalty and trust. In Vlad's case, his use of fear was effective because it was **calculated** and **targeted**, focusing on those who broke the law or posed a threat to his rule.

Rulers who rely solely on fear without balancing it with fairness often find that their reigns are **short-lived**. Fear can suppress dissent for a time, but without a sense of **justice or legitimacy**, it eventually leads to **discontent** and rebellion. Vlad's success lay in his ability to maintain a delicate balance between fear and fairness, using fear to enforce obedience while ensuring that his subjects recognized his rule as **just and necessary** for their protection and the stability of the kingdom.

Conclusion

VLAD THE IMPALER'S reign offers valuable insights into the **balance between fear and fairness** in governance. While fear played a critical role in maintaining control and deterring rebellion, Vlad also understood that **fairness and justice** were essential for securing **long-term loyalty** and stability. His ability to blend **ruthless punishment with impartial law enforcement** allowed him to create an atmosphere where disloyalty was swiftly punished, but law-abiding citizens were protected and governed fairly.

By striking this balance, Vlad maintained **legitimacy** in the eyes of his people, even as he ruled through fear. His reign demonstrates that effective governance requires more than just instilling fear—it requires a ruler to apply **fairness** in the enforcement of laws, ensuring that power is exercised not through cruelty alone but through **justice** that serves the greater good of the realm.

Chapter 8: The Cost of Ruthless Leadership

Ruthless leadership, while effective in securing power and maintaining order, often comes with significant costs. Leaders like Vlad the Impaler, who relied on **brutality, fear, and swift justice** to control their territories, may achieve **short-term stability** but risk alienating allies, breeding resentment among their people, and ultimately undermining the very foundations of their rule. While Vlad's harsh methods allowed him to repel external threats and suppress internal rebellion, the legacy of his **ruthless leadership** left deep scars on Wallachia.

The price of such leadership is often paid in **long-term instability**. Brutality creates fear, but fear does not build loyalty or lasting support. Those who are ruled by terror may obey, but they do so out of necessity, not devotion. Over time, the toll of this fear-driven leadership can create an undercurrent of **resentment**, both among the ruled and neighboring powers, leading to betrayal, isolation, and ultimately the downfall of even the most powerful rulers. This chapter explores the **consequences** of Vlad's ruthless leadership, examining how his reliance on terror solidified his power in the short term but sowed the seeds of future challenges and opposition.

Examining the personal and political costs of Vlad's methods

VLAD THE IMPALER'S leadership style, characterized by **ruthlessness and terror**, was undeniably effective in achieving immediate control over Wallachia and in defending his territory from external threats. However, the personal and political costs of his methods were profound, leaving lasting impacts not only on his reign but also on the region's future. While Vlad's use of **brutal tactics** allowed him to consolidate power and suppress rebellion, it also created **resentment**, isolation, and eventual instability that would haunt his rule and legacy.

1. The Political Isolation

ONE OF THE MOST SIGNIFICANT political costs of Vlad's leadership was his growing **isolation from potential allies**. His reliance on brutality and fear may have been effective in Wallachia, but it alienated many of the powerful figures within the region and across Europe. Vlad's extreme methods, particularly his infamous use of **impalement**, horrified many of his contemporaries, including neighboring Christian rulers, who might have otherwise been natural allies in the fight against the Ottoman Empire.

Rather than being seen as a heroic defender of Christendom, Vlad's **reputation for cruelty** made him a figure of fear and suspicion. Even **King Matthias Corvinus of Hungary**, who had supported Vlad at various points in his reign, eventually distanced himself from the voivode, imprisoning him for a time when it became politically expedient to do so. Vlad's methods, while effective in **defending Wallachia**, created an atmosphere where **foreign support dwindled**. His isolation was a direct result of his **ruthless reputation**, which made it difficult to maintain **lasting alliances**.

2. Internal Resentment and Opposition

VLAD'S BRUTAL LEADERSHIP also fostered **internal resentment** within Wallachia. His harsh punishments, while successful in quelling immediate threats, left a legacy of **fear and hatred** among the nobility, particularly the boyars, whom he often targeted. Many of the powerful families Vlad had purged or punished for treachery would nurse **long-standing grievances** against him. While his rule was marked by stability during his lifetime, the **seeds of rebellion** were sown by the **cruelty** he inflicted upon the nobility and other influential figures.

Even among the common people, the constant state of fear may have secured **obedience**, but it did not foster loyalty. While Vlad's strict laws against crime and corruption were seen as fair in some respects, his extreme methods meant that the line between **justice and tyranny** was often blurred. Fear kept dissent at bay, but it also meant that his people were unlikely to feel a sense of **devotion** to their ruler. This underlying **resentment** created an unstable foundation, one that would unravel after his death, when Wallachia became vulnerable to renewed internal strife and external invasion.

3. Personal Alienation and Paranoia

VLAD'S USE OF FEAR to secure his rule came with a significant **personal cost**. Constantly surrounded by enemies and potential traitors, Vlad's leadership was marked by a growing sense of **paranoia**. His own experiences of betrayal—by the boyars who had killed his father and brother, by allies who shifted their loyalties, and by external forces like the Ottomans—led him to adopt a **worldview shaped by suspicion and vengeance**.

This paranoia manifested in his increasingly **merciless actions**. Vlad saw threats everywhere and responded with swift and brutal reprisals, often executing or punishing individuals on suspicion alone. Over time, this isolated Vlad from those around him, as even his closest allies knew that they could easily fall out of favor. His **inability to**

trust anyone led him to rule through **force and fear**, creating an environment where true loyalty was hard to come by.

Vlad's personal alienation also extended to his relations with neighboring rulers. His brutal reputation preceded him, making it difficult for him to cultivate lasting relationships based on mutual trust and respect. His political isolation, combined with his personal paranoia, meant that Vlad was constantly under siege—both physically and psychologically—throughout his reign.

4. Reputation and Legacy

VLAD'S LEADERSHIP LEFT him with a **complex and divisive legacy**. While he is remembered in Romanian folklore as a strong, protective ruler who stood against foreign invaders, particularly the Ottoman Turks, his **brutal methods** also made him a notorious figure in European history. His reputation as a **ruthless, bloodthirsty tyrant** spread far beyond Wallachia, fueled by pamphlets and accounts that depicted him as a **monstrous figure** who impaled thousands of his enemies.

This reputation has had lasting consequences for how Vlad is remembered. While his brutality was effective in **defending Wallachia** and maintaining internal control, it also overshadowed his political achievements and diplomatic efforts. His name became synonymous with **cruelty**, and his legacy is often viewed through the lens of fear and violence, rather than as a ruler who attempted to stabilize a tumultuous region. His **historical reputation** has complicated the way he is understood, leaving him as both a **national hero** and a **global symbol of ruthless leadership**.

5. Long-term Instability After His Death

THE MOST PROFOUND POLITICAL cost of Vlad's leadership was the **long-term instability** that followed his death. While Vlad's brutal methods succeeded in keeping Wallachia united and secure during his lifetime, the **repressive environment** he created could not last once his presence was gone. The same nobility he had kept in check through fear would quickly regain power after his death, leading to renewed **infighting and factionalism**. Without a strong and feared leader like Vlad to enforce order, Wallachia became vulnerable once again to **internal strife** and **external domination**, particularly by the Ottoman Empire.

His failure to **build lasting institutions of governance** or cultivate genuine loyalty among his people left a power vacuum, as there was no clear successor who could rule with the same authority. The **fear-driven governance** that had sustained Vlad's rule did not leave a stable foundation for the future. Instead, Wallachia fell into further political turbulence, proving that **ruthless leadership**, while effective in the short term, often leaves a legacy of **division and instability**.

Conclusion

WHILE VLAD THE IMPALER'S use of **ruthless tactics** secured his power and protected Wallachia from both internal and external threats during his reign, the **personal and political costs** of his methods were undeniable. His reliance on **fear and brutality** left him **isolated** both politically and personally, alienating potential allies and fostering **resentment** among the nobility and common people alike. This isolation, combined with the long-term consequences of ruling through terror, left Wallachia vulnerable after his death, as his leadership style did not create a sustainable framework for stability.

In examining the cost of ruthless leadership, Vlad's reign provides a stark reminder that while **brutality can be effective in securing immediate power**, it often comes at the expense of **long-term stability** and **lasting legacy**. Fear alone cannot build loyalty, and in the absence of fairness and trust, ruthless leadership can sow the seeds of **future unrest** and **political isolation**.

How ruthlessness can secure power, but also lead to enemies and isolation

RUTHLESSNESS IN LEADERSHIP, while a powerful tool for securing control and deterring opposition, can often have profound consequences that extend beyond the immediate benefits of instilling fear and maintaining order. Leaders like Vlad the Impaler demonstrated how **ruthlessness** can effectively **consolidate power**, eliminate threats, and deter rebellion through swift and brutal punishment. However, this reliance on terror often comes with a significant cost: the creation of **enemies**, both internal and external, and eventual **isolation**, leaving the ruler vulnerable once fear alone is no longer enough to sustain control.

Ruthless methods can suppress dissent and crush rebellion in the short term, but they also breed **resentment, fear, and mistrust**. Over time, the very tactics that secure power may lead to **alienation** from allies, a lack of true loyalty among followers, and an environment in which **enemies multiply**, waiting for the opportune moment to strike. This dual-edged nature of ruthlessness underscores its utility as a temporary solution for maintaining power, but also highlights its inherent risks when used as the foundation of long-term governance.

1. Securing Power Through Ruthlessness

RUTHLESSNESS IS OFTEN the most direct way to **assert control** in times of chaos or when facing significant threats. For Vlad the Impaler, who ruled in a volatile region surrounded by hostile powers and disloyal nobles, **brutal and decisive action** was necessary to prevent his enemies from gaining the upper hand. His use of **mass impalements, public executions**, and other cruel punishments quickly established his reputation as a leader who would not tolerate disobedience or rebellion.

Vlad's ability to secure power through fear was evident in his **swift elimination of internal threats**. When he invited the boyars to the infamous **Easter feast**, only to execute or enslave many of them for their past betrayals, Vlad sent a clear message that disloyalty would be met with extreme consequences. This act of **ruthless justice** immediately weakened the power of the nobility, who had historically undermined Wallachian rulers, and solidified his control over the region.

Through his **brutal tactics**, Vlad was able to **suppress rebellion** and prevent future challenges to his authority. His reliance on **fear as a deterrent** made potential conspirators think twice before acting against him, and his willingness to punish even minor offenses harshly ensured that **law and order** were maintained. In this way, ruthlessness allowed Vlad to **consolidate power** quickly and efficiently, instilling both fear and respect among his subjects and enemies alike.

2. The Creation of Enemies

HOWEVER, THE VERY **ruthlessness** that allowed Vlad to secure power also contributed to the creation of **enemies**—both within his own ranks and among neighboring powers. His extreme methods of punishment, while effective in the short term, left many of the nobles and other influential figures in Wallachia nursing deep **resentments**. The boyars, in particular, who had suffered mass executions and the loss of their power, harbored long-standing grievances against Vlad, waiting for the right moment to act against him.

Even those who remained loyal to Vlad did so out of **fear, not devotion**. This lack of genuine loyalty meant that as soon as his power began to wane, those who had been kept in line through terror would turn against him, either out of self-preservation or revenge. The absence of a **trust-based relationship** between ruler and ruled made Vlad's position precarious, with many seeking to undermine his authority the moment the opportunity arose.

Externally, Vlad's **ruthless reputation** as a brutal and unpredictable leader made it difficult for him to maintain lasting alliances. His treatment of Ottoman envoys, who he impaled for perceived disrespect, and his merciless methods of repelling invasions, while successful militarily, alienated potential allies such as **Hungary and other Christian powers**. Neighboring rulers, who might have seen Vlad as a valuable ally in the fight against the Ottoman Empire, became wary of his extreme tactics, viewing him as a dangerous and volatile figure. This contributed to his **political isolation**, weakening his position on the international stage and leaving him vulnerable to **foreign intervention** and betrayal.

3. Political Isolation and Vulnerability

AS VLAD'S REIGN CONTINUED, the **consequences of his ruthless leadership** became more apparent in the form of **political isolation**. His extreme methods, which initially secured his power, made it difficult for him to cultivate and maintain **diplomatic relationships**. His brutal reputation spread far and wide, reaching the courts of neighboring rulers and European powers who saw Vlad not as a potential ally, but as a **tyrant** whose methods were too extreme to justify political support.

One of the clearest examples of Vlad's **isolation** came when **King Matthias Corvinus of Hungary**, who had previously supported Vlad's efforts to resist the Ottomans, eventually imprisoned him. Matthias, facing pressure from the Papacy and European powers to focus on uniting Christian forces against the Ottomans, distanced himself from Vlad, who had become politically toxic due to his **notorious reputation**. Vlad's ruthlessness had not only alienated him from his own people but also from those who might have helped him maintain his position in the broader geopolitical landscape.

This **isolation left Vlad vulnerable** to betrayal and opposition. Without strong alliances or loyal internal factions, he found himself increasingly reliant on fear alone to maintain power. When **enemies inside and outside** his kingdom sensed weakness, they were quick to act. His enemies, many of whom had been created by his brutal methods, began to **conspire against him**, leading to his eventual imprisonment and the loss of his throne.

4. Fear Without Loyalty: The Fragility of Ruthless Rule

THE PRIMARY FLAW OF a **ruthless leadership style** is that it often lacks the **foundation of loyalty and trust** necessary for long-term stability. While fear can secure obedience, it cannot foster genuine allegiance or devotion. In Vlad's case, his subjects, nobles, and even allies obeyed him largely out of fear for their lives rather than respect for his leadership. This meant that once the **fear began to fade**, either due to external pressure or internal weakness, there was little to sustain his rule.

Vlad's reliance on **brutal enforcement of power** made it difficult for him to build a **sustainable system of governance**. His rule was highly dependent on his personal presence and the fear he inspired; once removed from the equation, there were no enduring institutions or loyal power structures that could maintain control in his absence. This fragility became apparent after his imprisonment and eventual death, when **Wallachia fell into further instability** and became vulnerable to external domination.

Fear-driven leadership also creates an atmosphere of **constant vigilance**, where the leader must continuously reinforce their power through acts of brutality to prevent dissent. This cycle of terror can become exhausting and unsustainable over time, leading to **mental strain** on the ruler and a constant sense of paranoia about the loyalty of those around them. For Vlad, this meant that his reign was defined by **isolation and suspicion**, as he could never fully trust those closest to him, knowing that fear alone was the basis of their allegiance.

5. The Legacy of Ruthlessness

WHILE RUTHLESSNESS can be a powerful tool for **short-term success**, it often leaves a **dark and unstable legacy**. Vlad's reign, though effective in deterring rebellion and repelling enemies, left Wallachia in a state of **long-term instability**. The very people he had crushed through terror became the forces that contributed to his downfall, and after his death, the kingdom descended into renewed **internal strife** and **external threats**. The cost of securing power through ruthlessness was the inability to establish a **lasting, stable foundation** for the future.

In the end, **ruthless leadership** often creates as many enemies as it eliminates, leaving rulers isolated, vulnerable, and dependent on fear to maintain their grip on power. Vlad's reign illustrates how ruthlessness can be effective in achieving immediate control but also carries significant risks, leading to the **alienation of allies, the creation of enemies, and eventual political and personal isolation**.

Conclusion

VLAD THE IMPALER'S leadership demonstrates the **paradox of ruthlessness**: while it can secure power swiftly and decisively, it often leads to the creation of **enemies and political isolation**. Ruthlessness, by its nature, alienates those who might otherwise be allies and fosters an environment of fear that, over time, erodes trust and loyalty. Vlad's brutal methods allowed him to maintain control in a volatile region, but they also ensured that he would be surrounded by **enemies, both internal and external**, who waited for the right moment to strike. His reign serves as a reminder that **fear alone cannot sustain power indefinitely**, and without a balance of **loyalty and trust**, even the most ruthless leaders will eventually face the consequences of their methods.

What modern leaders can learn about the consequences of using fear

THE LESSONS FROM VLAD the Impaler's reign, particularly his use of fear as a tool of control, provide valuable insights for **modern leaders**. While fear can be an effective short-term strategy for achieving compliance, **ruling through fear alone** comes with significant risks and **long-term consequences**. Modern leaders, whether in politics, business, or other spheres, must understand the **complexity of fear-based leadership** and the potential costs associated with relying on fear to maintain power and influence.

Fear can bring **immediate results**: it can deter opposition, suppress dissent, and force quick compliance. However, as Vlad's reign illustrates, fear does not build **loyalty**, **trust**, or **lasting stability**. The use of fear can lead to **resentment, alienation**, and an eventual collapse of authority when fear no longer holds the same power. Modern leaders can learn several critical lessons from the **consequences of using fear**:

1. Fear May Secure Immediate Compliance, But It Does Not Build Loyalty

ONE OF THE KEY LESSONS modern leaders can learn is that while **fear can secure immediate results**, it does not foster genuine **loyalty or commitment**. When people follow out of fear, they are doing so to avoid consequences, not because they believe in the leader's vision or respect their authority. This lack of loyalty can lead to **instability** in the long run.

In the modern world, leaders who rule through fear might experience temporary success in getting employees, followers, or constituents to comply, but as soon as the source of fear is removed, the foundation of their leadership can crumble. Fear-based leadership

erodes trust over time, making it difficult for leaders to inspire genuine commitment to their goals or vision.

2. Fear Creates a Culture of Distrust and Isolation

ANOTHER CONSEQUENCE of using fear is the creation of a **culture of distrust**. Just as Vlad's brutal methods left him politically isolated and surrounded by enemies, modern leaders who rely on fear risk **alienating those around them**. A fearful environment encourages **self-preservation** over collaboration, with individuals more focused on protecting themselves from the leader's wrath than on working toward common goals.

In organizations or political systems, fear-based leadership often leads to **silos, secrecy, and a lack of open communication**. Team members may hide problems, avoid taking risks, or fail to innovate for fear of being punished. This stifles creativity and limits the leader's ability to adapt and grow, ultimately undermining the organization's long-term success. Additionally, leaders who use fear may find themselves increasingly **isolated** as their followers become more focused on avoiding conflict than on providing honest feedback or support.

3. Fear Is Unsustainable Over Time

ONE OF THE MOST IMPORTANT lessons modern leaders can learn is that **fear is not a sustainable leadership strategy**. While fear can be effective in the short term, its impact diminishes over time as people either grow accustomed to the threat or seek ways to subvert the leader's authority. In Vlad's case, the fear he instilled was powerful, but it created a fragile structure of power that quickly collapsed once he was no longer able to reinforce it.

In the modern context, leaders who rely on fear may find that their **influence wanes** as their followers either become resistant to fear-based tactics or find ways to undermine the leader's control. As the fear fades, the **underlying resentment** that has built up may lead to **rebellion, disengagement, or departure** from the organization. In business or political environments, this can result in **high turnover**, **lack of engagement**, or **mass opposition**, all of which can destabilize the leader's position.

4. Fear Can Lead to Unintended Consequences

USING FEAR AS A TOOL of leadership often results in **unintended consequences**, as people respond in ways that may be unpredictable or counterproductive. For example, fear may push individuals to take **shortcuts, cover up mistakes**, or even engage in **deceptive practices** to avoid punishment. These behaviors can undermine the integrity of the organization or system and lead to larger issues down the road.

In the political sphere, ruling through fear can lead to **increased opposition** and **resistance** from those who feel oppressed. Fear may force temporary compliance, but it also breeds **hatred and resentment**, which can manifest in **revolts, protests**, or even **violent resistance**. In the modern world, where information spreads rapidly and movements can gain momentum quickly, the consequences of fear-based leadership can be difficult to contain.

5. Leaders Must Balance Fear with Fairness and Trust

A CRITICAL LESSON FOR modern leaders is the need to **balance fear with fairness and trust**. While some level of **authority and discipline** is necessary for leadership, it must be accompanied by **fair treatment** and **ethical governance**. Without fairness, fear becomes oppression, and people will resist rather than follow.

Modern leaders can benefit from creating environments where **accountability** exists, but where **trust** and **transparency** are equally valued. By establishing clear rules and enforcing them fairly, leaders can maintain authority without relying solely on fear. In such environments, people follow not because they are afraid of punishment but because they **trust the leader's vision and believe in their integrity**.

6. Fear-Based Leadership Hinders Innovation and Growth

FEAR STIFLES **creativity, innovation, and risk-taking**—all of which are essential for the growth of organizations, nations, and teams. When people are afraid of making mistakes or stepping out of line, they are less likely to propose new ideas or take the kind of calculated risks that lead to breakthroughs. In the business world, this can prevent companies from **innovating** or responding to new challenges in a competitive marketplace.

For modern leaders, fostering an environment where **learning from failure** is accepted and even encouraged is crucial. Leaders who use fear discourage experimentation, leading to **stagnation**. In contrast, leaders who cultivate **trust** and **psychological safety** empower their followers to think creatively and solve problems collaboratively, which is key to long-term success.

7. True Leadership Is Built on Respect, Not Fear

ONE OF THE MOST IMPORTANT lessons modern leaders can take away from the consequences of fear-based leadership is that **respect is a far more powerful and enduring foundation for leadership than fear**. Respect is built through **consistent, fair, and transparent leadership**, where followers know they are valued, listened to, and treated with integrity. When people respect their leader, they are more likely to go the extra mile, remain loyal, and support the leader through difficult times.

Leaders who inspire respect are able to foster a sense of **shared purpose and commitment**, which is far more resilient than the compliance generated through fear. In the long run, **respect-based**

leadership creates **loyalty, trust, and stability**, all of which are essential for enduring success in any field.

Conclusion

THE LEGACY OF **fear-based leadership** offers important lessons for modern leaders. While fear can be an effective tool for gaining **short-term compliance**, it comes with long-term costs, including **resentment, isolation, and instability**. Modern leaders must recognize that **fear alone is not a sustainable leadership strategy**. Instead, they should strive to balance authority with **fairness, trust, and respect**, creating environments where people feel empowered, valued, and motivated to work toward common goals.

By avoiding the pitfalls of fear-driven leadership and focusing on **ethical governance, open communication**, and **inspiring respect**, modern leaders can build **lasting influence and loyalty**, ensuring that their leadership is resilient and capable of withstanding the challenges of an ever-changing world.

Chapter 9: The Fall of Vlad the Impaler

The downfall of Vlad the Impaler is a cautionary tale about the limits of **ruthless leadership** and the dangers of ruling through fear alone. While his reign had been marked by brutal methods that secured control over Wallachia and deterred enemies, the very strategies that allowed Vlad to maintain power also contributed to his eventual **fall from grace**. His reliance on terror created **enemies on all sides**, from disloyal nobles at home to external powers that saw his cruelty as a liability.

Vlad's **political isolation**, fueled by his harsh treatment of allies and enemies alike, left him vulnerable when the tides turned against him. His imprisonment by the Hungarian king and eventual death in battle reflect the inevitable consequences of ruling without building lasting alliances or fostering loyalty among those he ruled. The fall of Vlad the Impaler demonstrates the fragility of **fear-based governance** and the ultimate cost of relying solely on **brutality and intimidation** to maintain power.

Vlad's eventual downfall and the political machinations that led to his death

THE FALL OF VLAD THE Impaler was not the result of any single battle or decisive defeat, but rather a culmination of **political machinations, betrayal, and shifting alliances**. Despite his fierce leadership and ability to hold off enemies like the Ottoman Empire, Vlad's **reliance on brutality** and fear ultimately left him isolated and vulnerable to the very forces he had sought to control. His downfall was marked by the treacherous nature of the political environment in Wallachia, Hungary, and the surrounding regions, where **alliances shifted rapidly** and loyalty was often fleeting.

1. Imprisonment by King Matthias Corvinus

ONE OF THE MOST SIGNIFICANT turning points in Vlad's downfall was his **imprisonment by King Matthias Corvinus of Hungary**. Early in his reign, Matthias had supported Vlad in his efforts to defend Wallachia against the Ottomans, seeing him as a useful ally in the struggle to keep the Ottoman forces at bay. However, Vlad's reputation for **brutality** and his increasingly isolated political stance became problematic, particularly as Europe sought to unite Christian forces against the Ottoman threat.

In 1462, after successfully repelling an Ottoman invasion with his **guerrilla tactics** and infamous **Night Attack**, Vlad sought refuge in Hungary. However, instead of providing support, King Matthias had Vlad **imprisoned**. This decision was partly due to Matthias's need to maintain good relations with other European powers and the Papacy, both of which were disturbed by Vlad's methods. The **Ottoman propaganda** against Vlad, which depicted him as a bloodthirsty tyrant, further complicated Matthias's position, making it politically expedient to distance himself from the Wallachian voivode.

Matthias used the pretext of Vlad's alleged **betrayal of Christian interests** to justify his imprisonment, despite the fact that Vlad had remained a staunch opponent of Ottoman expansion. The decision to imprison Vlad was a calculated move on Matthias's part, driven by **political necessity** and the desire to maintain diplomatic favor with Western powers, as well as the growing unpopularity of Vlad's harsh rule.

2. Internal Rebellion and Nobility's Revenge

VLAD'S BRUTAL SUPPRESSION of the **Wallachian boyars**—the noble class who had long held significant power—was a key element of his strategy for maintaining control. However, this ruthlessness also earned him **lasting enemies** among the nobility, many of whom harbored deep **resentment** for the executions, mass impalements, and forced labor Vlad had imposed upon them. These nobles, who had been biding their time for revenge, seized upon Vlad's imprisonment as an opportunity to restore their influence.

During his imprisonment, **internal rebellion** spread through Wallachia, led by the very nobles Vlad had oppressed. They sought to install a new ruler, often backed by the **Ottoman Empire** or **Hungary**, depending on who could provide the most advantageous support. Vlad's absence created a **power vacuum** that was quickly filled by rival factions, each eager to undo the centralized control Vlad had imposed. The boyars' return to power after his imprisonment was not just an act of rebellion, but one of **retribution**, aimed at dismantling the system Vlad had brutally enforced.

3. Shifting Allegiances and Ottoman Involvement

THE GEOPOLITICAL SITUATION in Eastern Europe during Vlad's time was fluid, with **alliances shifting constantly** between regional powers such as Hungary, the Ottoman Empire, and even Poland. Vlad's relationship with the **Ottoman Sultan Mehmed II** was especially complicated. While Vlad had openly defied Ottoman demands for tribute and launched raids into their territory, there were moments when pragmatism dictated more diplomatic interactions. Nevertheless, the Ottomans viewed Vlad as a serious threat to their interests in Wallachia, and his **defiance** did not go unnoticed.

After his imprisonment, the Ottomans began backing **Radu the Handsome**, Vlad's younger brother, who had been loyal to the Ottoman court during his earlier captivity. With Ottoman support, Radu took the throne of Wallachia, and Vlad's once-firm grip on the region was effectively broken. Radu's more **pro-Ottoman stance** allowed the empire to exert greater control over Wallachia, further marginalizing Vlad's position.

Vlad's eventual release from imprisonment in 1475 was due to shifting political dynamics once again. As tensions with the Ottomans escalated, Matthias Corvinus found it strategically advantageous to **reinstate Vlad** as a ruler who could resist Ottoman encroachment. However, this return to power was brief, as Vlad's enemies had not forgotten his earlier cruelties, and he remained a **divisive figure** in Wallachian politics.

4. Final Campaign and Death in Battle

IN 1476, VLAD EMBARKED on a final campaign to reclaim his throne with the support of Hungarian forces and the **Moldavian prince Stephen the Great**. Vlad was able to retake Wallachia for a short period, but the situation remained volatile. The Ottomans, now firmly allied with many of the Wallachian boyars and Radu's supporters, sought to remove him once and for all. Vlad's attempt to rebuild his power base was met with significant resistance from the boyars who had grown accustomed to their renewed influence and the **Ottoman-aligned factions** that saw him as a threat to their stability.

Vlad's downfall ultimately came during a battle with Ottoman-backed forces in late 1476. Accounts of his death are varied, but it is generally accepted that he was **killed in battle**, possibly betrayed by his own men or ambushed by Ottoman forces. Some stories suggest that his head was cut off and sent to Sultan Mehmed II as proof of his death. Others imply that **internal betrayal** played a role, with former allies turning on Vlad at the last moment to secure favor with the Ottomans or other regional powers.

5. Legacy of Ruthless Leadership

VLAD'S DEATH MARKED the end of his turbulent reign, but his legacy lived on as both a **national hero** who defended Wallachia from foreign domination and as a **ruthless tyrant** who ruled through fear and brutality. His downfall illustrates the inherent risks of **ruling through terror**, where alliances are fragile, enemies are numerous, and trust is nonexistent. The very methods that allowed him to maintain power ultimately created the conditions for his demise, as **political isolation** and the accumulation of enemies made it impossible for him to hold onto power in the long run.

His reliance on brutality not only alienated potential allies but also ensured that **internal factions** would rise up against him as soon as the opportunity presented itself. Vlad's eventual fall underscores the limitations of ruling through fear alone—while effective in the short term, it left him with **few true supporters** and many waiting for the moment to bring him down.

Conclusion

VLAD THE IMPALER'S eventual downfall was the result of **political machinations, shifting alliances,** and the accumulation of enemies both within and outside Wallachia. His reliance on **brutal tactics** and fear-based rule may have secured his position for a time, but it also alienated key figures and left him vulnerable when the political winds shifted. Betrayed, imprisoned, and eventually killed in battle, Vlad's demise illustrates the precarious nature of **ruling through**

ruthlessness, where the very forces used to maintain power can become the agents of a leader's destruction.

Analysis of Vlad the Impaler's legacy in Romania and his place in world history

VLAD THE IMPALER, KNOWN locally as **Vlad Țepeș** or Vlad Dracul, holds a unique and complex position in both **Romanian history** and **world history**. His legacy is shaped by a duality that reflects the turbulent times he lived in: on one hand, he is seen as a **national hero** who fiercely defended Wallachia from foreign invasion and preserved its independence against the Ottoman Empire. On the other hand, his reputation as a **brutal ruler** who employed extreme methods of punishment, particularly impalement, has cast him as a figure of **fear and cruelty** in the broader historical narrative.

Vlad's legacy is further complicated by his association with **Bram Stoker's Dracula**, which, while historically inaccurate, has contributed to his enduring presence in global popular culture. This analysis explores the **two-sided legacy** of Vlad the Impaler: how he is viewed in Romania as a defender of his people and his enduring, albeit distorted, place in world history as a symbol of **ruthlessness and horror**.

1. Vlad the National Hero: Defender of Wallachia

IN ROMANIA, VLAD THE Impaler is remembered primarily as a **defender of the nation**, a figure who protected Wallachia from the constant threat of Ottoman expansion. During the 15th century, Wallachia was caught between two great powers: the **Ottoman Empire** to the south and the **Kingdom of Hungary** to the north. Vlad's reign was marked by his staunch resistance to Ottoman dominance, particularly his refusal to pay tribute to the Sultan, which led to multiple military confrontations.

His most famous military action, the **Night Attack of 1462**, where he launched a surprise raid on the Ottoman camp, is celebrated as an example of his **strategic genius** and **bravery** in the face of overwhelming odds. Vlad's guerrilla tactics and scorched-earth policies, while brutal, are seen as necessary measures to **defend Wallachian sovereignty**. He is often compared to other Eastern European rulers, such as **Stephen the Great of Moldavia**, who similarly fought to preserve their lands from foreign domination.

In Romanian culture, Vlad's **harsh methods** are interpreted through the lens of **justice** rather than cruelty. His impalement of enemies and disloyal nobles, while horrifying to outsiders, is seen as a means of restoring **order** in a time of widespread lawlessness and corruption. Romanian folklore often portrays him as a **vigilante ruler** who stood up to the wealthy and powerful boyars, punished criminals, and sought to bring **fairness and security** to his people. This narrative positions Vlad as a **symbol of Romanian resistance** and a protector of national identity, making him a **heroic figure** in the country's history.

2. The Brutal Tyrant: His Place in Global History

WHILE VLAD IS REVERED in Romania, his **international legacy** is dominated by his reputation as a **ruthless tyrant**. His infamous use of **impalement** as a method of execution and intimidation shocked contemporaries and has been central to his portrayal in world history. Contemporary accounts of Vlad's reign, particularly from foreign sources such as German and Hungarian pamphlets, emphasized the **gruesome details** of his rule, portraying him as a sadistic despot who reveled in cruelty.

These accounts, while often exaggerated for political purposes, contributed to Vlad's long-standing reputation in the West as a **monster in human form**. His brutal treatment of both internal and external enemies, his mass impalements, and his reputation for **psychological terror** made him one of the most feared rulers of his time. This portrayal of Vlad as a **bloodthirsty ruler** is part of what has cemented his place in the broader global historical narrative as a symbol of **authoritarian cruelty**.

Moreover, his methods of punishment were often seen as extreme, even for the standards of his time, contributing to his reputation as a **figure of terror**. The association of his name with **vampirism** through **Bram Stoker's Dracula** further entrenched this legacy. While Stoker's novel is not a direct retelling of Vlad's life, the choice of the name **"Dracula"** (derived from Vlad's father's title, "Dracul," meaning "Dragon") has linked Vlad forever with the **fictional vampire**, casting a shadow over his historical achievements.

3. The Dracula Myth: Fiction and History Intertwined

VLAD THE IMPALER'S **association with the Dracula myth** has significantly shaped his legacy in global popular culture. **Bram Stoker's 1897 novel** *Dracula* drew loosely on the historical figure of Vlad, transforming him into a **supernatural villain** who preys on the living, adding a **gothic dimension** to the historical Vlad's reputation for bloodshed. Stoker's Dracula is not meant to be a direct representation of Vlad the Impaler, but the connection between the two has grown stronger over time, leading to a blending of fact and fiction.

This mythologized version of Vlad has played a significant role in the way the world views him, turning him into a figure of **horror and fantasy**. While Vlad's historical role as a ruler who defended his kingdom is well-documented, his **Dracula association** has led to an almost **sensationalized version** of his legacy, where his actual achievements are often overshadowed by his fictional counterpart. Today, Vlad the Impaler is as likely to be remembered as **Dracula, the vampire count** as he is for his historical role as the voivode of Wallachia.

Despite the **fictional nature of the Dracula myth**, the association has had real consequences for how Vlad is remembered. The **tourism industry** in Romania has capitalized on the Dracula connection, with many visitors coming to explore sites linked to both the historical Vlad and the fictional vampire. This has kept Vlad's name alive in **global** consciousness, but often through the lens of **gothic horror** rather than historical reality.

4. Balancing Heroism and Brutality

VLAD THE IMPALER'S legacy is one of **contradiction**: he is both a **national hero** and a **global villain**, a **defender of his people** and a **tyrant feared for his cruelty**. In Romania, efforts to reclaim Vlad's legacy as a **protector of Wallachia** often clash with the broader world's view of him as a figure of terror. For Romanians, Vlad's brutality is contextualized as necessary for the defense of his land during a period of **constant threat from powerful empires**.

Globally, however, Vlad is often seen through a more negative lens. His use of **fear as a weapon**, his punishment of enemies and nobles, and his methods of enforcing authority make him a figure who symbolizes the dangers of **authoritarian rule**. Vlad's reign offers a powerful example of how **brutality can secure power**, but it also serves as a reminder of the long-term costs of ruling through fear and terror.

5. Vlad's Place in World History

VLAD THE IMPALER'S place in **world history** is a testament to the complexities of leadership in a **violent and unstable** time. As a historical figure, he represents the challenges faced by rulers of small states in maintaining independence against larger powers. His strategic brilliance, particularly in military tactics, and his ability to repel **Ottoman invasions** should not be overshadowed by his methods. Vlad is an example of how **leaders in times of crisis** may resort to extreme measures, but also of how these measures come to define their legacy in unpredictable ways.

In the broader scope of world history, Vlad is a symbol of **ruthless leadership** and the consequences of ruling through fear. His name evokes images of **tyranny and bloodshed**, a ruler who used terror to maintain control. Yet, his role as a **defender of Christendom** and as a leader who fought to protect his people from foreign domination remains an important part of his legacy. Vlad the Impaler stands as a **paradoxical figure**, remembered for both his **heroism** and his **cruelty**, with his legacy forever shaped by the tensions between these two sides of his rule.

Conclusion

VLAD THE IMPALER'S legacy is a complex one, marked by his **heroic defense of Wallachia** and his **reputation for extreme brutality**. In Romania, he is celebrated as a **national icon**, a ruler who stood against foreign oppression and brought order to a fractured land. Globally, however, Vlad's name is often associated with terror, cruelty, and the **myth of Dracula**. His place in world history is unique, standing at the intersection of **historical reality and gothic myth**, where his **military achievements** and **brutal tactics** are viewed through a lens of both admiration and horror.

Chapter 10: Leadership Lessons from Vlad the Impaler

Vlad the Impaler's reign offers a unique and complex set of **leadership lessons**, drawn from both his successes and his ultimate downfall. As a ruler, Vlad displayed exceptional **courage, strategic insight, and decisiveness**, qualities that helped him secure power in a dangerous and volatile region. However, his reliance on **ruthless tactics** and the use of fear as a primary tool of governance also reveal the **limitations and risks** of leading through brutality. His story serves as a powerful reminder that while **fear can control**, it does not build lasting loyalty or trust, and the consequences of relying solely on terror can be profound.

From Vlad's life, modern leaders can draw valuable insights into the **balance between strength and fairness**, the importance of **strategic decision-making**, and the dangers of **isolating oneself through fear-based rule**. This chapter will explore the **leadership lessons** that can be gleaned from Vlad's rise to power, his methods of governance, and the reasons behind his eventual downfall. Through this examination, key takeaways emerge about the need for **visionary leadership, ethical decision-making**, and **long-term strategies** that balance strength with wisdom.

Recap of key takeaways from Vlad's reign

VLAD THE IMPALER'S leadership offers a range of valuable lessons, reflecting both the strengths and pitfalls of his unique approach to governance. His reign, marked by **ruthless methods** and **military brilliance**, provides important insights into how leaders can secure power in difficult circumstances, but also reveals the potential long-term costs of relying on **fear and brutality** as primary tools of control. Here are the key takeaways from Vlad's reign:

1. Decisiveness in Leadership

VLAD WAS KNOWN FOR his ability to make **swift, decisive decisions**, particularly in times of crisis. Whether confronting internal rebellion or external invasion, he acted quickly to eliminate threats, often with ruthless efficiency. His decisiveness enabled him to maintain control over Wallachia, despite constant threats from both the nobility and the powerful Ottoman Empire. Modern leaders can learn the importance of **decisive action** in critical moments, but they must balance this with ethical considerations and the long-term impact of their decisions.

2. The Power of Fear

VLAD EFFECTIVELY USED **fear as a tool** to maintain control, deterring rebellion and securing obedience through brutal punishments like impalement. His reign illustrates that fear can be a powerful short-term strategy to eliminate opposition and enforce order. However, fear alone is not enough to build **lasting loyalty** or trust. Leaders who rely too heavily on fear risk alienating their followers and creating enemies, both inside and outside their sphere of influence.

3. Strategic Thinking and Military Tactics

VLAD WAS A MASTER OF **asymmetric warfare** and guerrilla tactics, successfully defending his kingdom from larger and more powerful enemies like the Ottoman Empire. His **Night Attack** against the Ottomans remains a famous example of his ability to use **strategy and terrain** to overcome overwhelming odds. Modern leaders, especially in complex or challenging environments, can learn from Vlad's ability to **adapt**, use limited resources effectively, and think strategically to outmaneuver stronger opponents.

4. The Risks of Isolation

WHILE VLAD'S BRUTAL tactics helped him gain control, they also **isolated him politically**. His ruthless treatment of the Wallachian nobility, and his alienation of potential allies like Hungary, left him vulnerable when political winds shifted. His imprisonment by King Matthias Corvinus is a clear example of how **isolation** can weaken even the most powerful leaders. Modern leaders must recognize the importance of building **strong alliances** and fostering **loyalty** rather than relying solely on fear and intimidation.

5. The Balance Between Fear and Fairness

VLAD'S ABILITY TO ENFORCE strict laws and punish corruption made him a **respected figure** among some of his subjects, especially the lower classes. His reign shows that **order and discipline** are important for maintaining control, but they must be tempered with **fairness** and **justice**. Leaders who are perceived as fair, even if harsh, are more likely to earn the respect and support of their followers. However, when fear overshadows fairness, resentment and opposition can grow, leading to instability.

6. The Consequences of Ruthless Leadership

WHILE VLAD'S RUTHLESS leadership secured power in the short term, it ultimately contributed to his downfall. His use of terror created enemies within Wallachia and abroad, leading to his eventual **political isolation** and death in battle. The lesson here is that **brutality** can win immediate victories, but it can also sow the seeds of future resistance. Leaders must be aware of the long-term consequences of their methods and avoid **alienating** those they need to sustain their power.

7. The Importance of Vision and Legacy

VLAD'S REIGN WAS MARKED by **short-term success**, but his inability to build lasting institutions or alliances meant that Wallachia struggled after his death. Modern leaders can learn the importance of **creating a sustainable vision** for the future, rather than relying on fear or personal charisma alone to maintain control. A leader's legacy is not just defined by their time in power, but by the systems and relationships they build that endure long after they are gone.

Conclusion

VLAD THE IMPALER'S reign offers **valuable leadership lessons** that remain relevant today. His decisiveness, strategic thinking, and ability to use fear to maintain control demonstrate the power of **strong leadership** in difficult circumstances. However, his reliance on fear and brutality, and the **political isolation** that resulted, serve as a warning of the dangers of ruling through terror alone. Modern leaders can learn from both Vlad's successes and his failures, recognizing the need to balance **strength with fairness, fear with loyalty,** and **short-term victories with long-term stability.**

How fear, power, and control can be applied in leadership today

WHILE **fear, power, and control** have been traditional tools for leadership, their application in the modern world requires careful consideration. In today's context, leadership that relies solely on fear is generally regarded as unsustainable and potentially damaging. However, when these elements are balanced with **ethical practices, transparency, and emotional intelligence**, they can still play a role in **effective leadership**. The key is not to wield fear, power, and control indiscriminately, but to use them **strategically and responsibly** in a way that drives results, maintains authority, and promotes long-term loyalty.

Here's how fear, power, and control can be applied in modern leadership:

1. Fear: Strategic Use for Setting Boundaries

WHILE FEAR-BASED LEADERSHIP in the traditional sense—ruling through terror—has largely been replaced by more collaborative and empathetic leadership models, **fear** still has a role in **setting boundaries** and ensuring that consequences are clearly understood. Leaders can leverage fear in a **calculated and controlled** manner to create accountability and uphold standards of behavior without crossing into tyranny.

- **Setting expectations**: Leaders can establish clear rules, expectations, and the consequences of non-compliance. The **fear of consequences**—such as losing a job, missing out on opportunities, or damaging reputation—can motivate individuals to meet goals and adhere to high standards.

- **Enforcing discipline**: In certain high-stakes situations, where failure to perform can have serious repercussions, invoking fear may be necessary to **impress the seriousness** of the situation. For instance, in high-risk industries (such as healthcare or military), the fear of making critical mistakes may drive **precision, caution, and discipline**.

However, this form of leadership must be used sparingly, as over-reliance on fear can create a **toxic culture** where employees feel unsafe, disengaged, or motivated to hide mistakes instead of learning from them. Leaders should focus on creating **accountability through transparency** and fairness rather than instilling constant fear.

2. Power: Leading with Authority and Integrity

POWER is an intrinsic part of leadership, but how power is exercised defines the effectiveness and sustainability of leadership. In the modern context, leaders must learn to wield power with **integrity and responsibility** while ensuring that it is used to **empower** rather than oppress.

- **Exercising authority responsibly**: Leaders should project confidence and decisiveness, using their power to **set direction, make tough decisions**, and provide a clear vision for the future. However, true authority comes from **earning respect** rather than demanding compliance. Power should be seen as a tool to **inspire action and unite teams** under a common goal, not as a means to intimidate or dominate.

- **Delegating power**: Modern leadership often involves the **distribution of power**, empowering others to take ownership of their roles and contribute to the overall success of the organization. Leaders who **delegate responsibility** and trust their team build a culture of **shared power** and collective success, which in turn strengthens their own authority.

- **Power through influence**: In today's leadership landscape, the ability to **influence others** is more important than exercising control through direct orders. Power through **persuasion, emotional intelligence, and inspiring loyalty** allows leaders to harness the strengths of their team without the need for coercion.

3. Control: Balancing Structure with Flexibility

CONTROL remains a necessary aspect of leadership, especially in terms of maintaining **structure, discipline, and focus** within an organization. However, modern leadership requires a balance between control and **flexibility**, ensuring that employees feel **empowered** rather than micromanaged.

- **Setting clear goals and accountability**: Leaders must maintain **control over outcomes** by setting **clear, measurable goals** and ensuring that everyone in the organization is aligned with the broader mission. Regular check-ins, performance reviews, and strategic oversight are tools of control that allow leaders to ensure progress without stifling creativity or autonomy.

- **Creating systems and processes**: Control also involves creating **efficient systems** and processes that allow for smooth operations and **consistent performance**. Leaders can establish structured workflows, decision-making processes, and communication channels to ensure that their teams are productive and aligned with organizational goals.

- **Balancing control with autonomy**: Today's workforce values **autonomy**, and leaders who allow room for **innovation** and individual initiative tend to foster more loyalty and creativity. The key is to provide **guidance and oversight**, but leave space for employees to own their work and contribute new ideas. Controlling the **framework** while allowing flexibility within it is the mark of an effective leader.

4. Applying These Concepts in Leadership Today

TO EFFECTIVELY APPLY **fear, power, and control** in modern leadership, these elements must be **redefined** for today's environment, ensuring that they align with values of **fairness, trust**, and **collaboration**. The combination of strength and emotional intelligence is key:

- **Building trust while maintaining authority**: Leaders must build **genuine relationships** with their teams, fostering **open communication** and trust, even as they maintain control and accountability. This approach ensures that authority is **respected** and not feared, and that team members feel supported rather than oppressed.

- **Using fear in a healthy way**: Leaders can create a healthy sense of **urgency or pressure** to meet deadlines or achieve goals without creating a toxic environment. Clear expectations, transparency, and the consistent enforcement of fair consequences help ensure that **fear of failure** motivates rather than paralyzes.

- **Empowering others through distributed power**: Leaders who share power by **delegating responsibility** and decision-making authority to trusted individuals or teams build **stronger, more resilient organizations.** Empowered employees are more likely to innovate and remain engaged, knowing they have the trust of their leadership.

5. Conclusion: A Balanced Approach

IN MODERN LEADERSHIP, the use of **fear, power, and control** must be **balanced with trust, transparency, and empowerment.** While fear can be used to establish boundaries and power is necessary for decision-making, **long-term success** depends on creating an environment where **loyalty is earned, not demanded,** and where control is paired with the freedom to innovate and grow. Leaders who skillfully combine these elements with **ethical leadership** and **empathy** will be more successful in navigating the complexities of today's leadership landscape.

The balance between strong leadership and maintaining moral boundaries

STRONG LEADERSHIP AND **moral integrity** are not mutually exclusive. In fact, the most effective leaders are those who balance **decisiveness and authority** with a deep commitment to **ethical principles**. In today's world, where leaders are constantly scrutinized by their teams, the public, and other stakeholders, maintaining moral boundaries is critical to building **lasting trust, credibility**, and **loyalty**. While strong leadership requires making difficult decisions and sometimes enforcing discipline, it must be done within a framework of **fairness, respect, and ethical behavior.**

Here's how leaders can strike the balance between **asserting authority** and **maintaining moral boundaries**:

1. Leading with Integrity

AT THE CORE OF MAINTAINING moral boundaries is **integrity**—the adherence to moral and ethical principles even when it is difficult or inconvenient. Leaders who operate with integrity inspire trust and confidence, making it easier to lead with strength while maintaining **credibility**.

- **Consistency in actions and values**: Strong leadership involves **aligning decisions and actions** with stated values. Leaders who demonstrate **consistency** between what they say and what they do set a clear example for their teams, showing that moral principles are non-negotiable, even in high-pressure situations.

- **Transparency and honesty**: Leaders should be **transparent** about their decision-making processes and openly communicate the reasons behind difficult decisions.

Even when enforcing discipline or navigating crises, being upfront fosters **trust** and signals that the leader's actions are grounded in ethical considerations.

2. Enforcing Accountability Without Losing Fairness

STRONG LEADERS MUST hold their teams accountable for their actions, but this must be done with **fairness** and **objectivity**. Leaders who are too punitive or arbitrary in their enforcement of rules risk losing moral authority, as well as the respect of their team members.

- **Clear and fair consequences**: Establishing **clear expectations** and consistent consequences for failing to meet those expectations is essential. However, consequences must be applied fairly, without favoritism or excessive harshness. Leaders should avoid relying on **fear** or punishment as their primary tools and instead create a culture where **accountability** is balanced with support for improvement.

- **Encouraging personal responsibility**: Instead of just enforcing punishment, strong leaders encourage individuals to take **personal responsibility** for their actions and learn from their mistakes. This helps maintain **moral boundaries** by focusing on **growth and development** rather than pure discipline.

3. Balancing Decisiveness with Empathy

ONE OF THE HALLMARKS of strong leadership is the ability to make **tough, decisive decisions**. However, these decisions should always be tempered with **empathy** and a genuine concern for the well-being of others.

- **Understanding the human impact of decisions**: Strong leaders recognize that every decision—whether it's a business strategy, restructuring, or disciplinary action—affects people's lives. Before making difficult choices, leaders should take the time to understand the **human impact** of their decisions and consider ways to mitigate harm wherever possible.

- **Empathy as a strength**: Some leaders mistakenly view **empathy** as a weakness. However, empathy is a powerful tool that allows leaders to **connect with their teams**, understand their needs, and make decisions that are both strong and compassionate. Leaders who exhibit empathy are often better able to navigate **complex challenges** without losing sight of their moral compass.

4. Building a Culture of Trust and Respect

TO BALANCE STRENGTH and moral boundaries, leaders need to foster a **culture of trust and mutual respect** within their organization. A strong leader does not need to rely on **intimidation** or control to command respect; instead, they build a **supportive environment** where individuals are motivated by shared values.

- **Leading by example**: Leaders set the tone for the entire organization, and those who demonstrate ethical behavior inspire others to do the same. **Leading by example** means adhering to moral boundaries, even when it's difficult, and consistently **modeling ethical behavior** in every decision.

- **Encouraging open dialogue**: Leaders should create spaces for **open communication** where employees feel safe to voice concerns, share ideas, and challenge decisions in a respectful manner. By welcoming feedback and engaging in

constructive dialogue, leaders build trust and ensure that moral boundaries are reinforced throughout the organization.

5. Making Tough Decisions Without Compromising Ethics

STRONG LEADERSHIP OFTEN requires making decisions that are unpopular or difficult, but moral boundaries should not be compromised in the process. Leaders who stay committed to **ethical principles** while navigating complex challenges are more likely to gain long-term respect, even if their decisions are initially controversial.

- **Long-term perspective**: Strong leaders take a **long-term view** when making decisions, considering not only the immediate outcomes but also the lasting impact on their organization's culture, reputation, and relationships. Leaders who prioritize short-term gains at the expense of ethical considerations often face **long-term consequences**, including loss of trust and credibility.

- **Courage to uphold moral principles**: It takes courage to stand by moral boundaries, especially in situations where cutting corners or compromising values might offer a quicker or easier solution. Strong leaders understand that their **moral integrity** is foundational to their leadership and are willing to make difficult decisions in order to uphold that integrity.

6. Adapting to Situational Needs Without Losing Integrity

SITUATIONAL LEADERSHIP involves adapting one's approach based on the specific circumstances at hand. However, even in rapidly changing or high-stakes situations, leaders must stay grounded in **core ethical principles**.

- **Flexibility without moral compromise**: While strong leaders must be flexible and adaptable, they should never bend their moral boundaries to suit the moment. True strength in leadership comes from the ability to **adapt strategies** and approaches without compromising on ethical principles. Leaders who maintain this balance inspire confidence and earn respect, even in challenging times.

- **Navigating crises with ethics intact**: Crises often push leaders to make swift, high-pressure decisions. Maintaining a **moral framework** during such times is critical. Strong leaders stay committed to doing what's **right**, even when faced with immense pressure to prioritize expediency over ethics.

Conclusion

THE BALANCE BETWEEN **strong leadership** and **moral boundaries** is critical to effective and sustainable leadership. While leaders must be assertive, decisive, and unafraid to make difficult decisions, those decisions must always be **grounded in ethical principles** and fairness. Leaders who combine strength with **integrity, empathy, and transparency** not only inspire loyalty and trust but also create lasting positive impacts on their organizations and those they lead.

By consistently upholding **moral boundaries**, even in challenging situations, strong leaders build **credibility** and leave a **legacy of ethical leadership**, demonstrating that true power lies in leading with both authority and integrity.

Conclusion: The Lasting Impact of Vlad the Impaler

A final reflection on how Vlad's leadership style has influenced history

Vlad the Impaler's leadership style, marked by **brutality, fear, and unwavering authority**, has left a lasting imprint on both **historical narratives** and **popular culture**. His reign offers a compelling example of how **ruthless leadership** can secure power in the short term but carries significant long-term consequences. While Vlad's ability to maintain control over Wallachia in the face of internal rebellion and external threats is impressive, the very tactics that made him a powerful ruler also isolated him, fostered resentment, and ultimately contributed to his downfall. His leadership style has influenced the way history remembers **authoritarian leaders**, particularly those who rule through **fear and intimidation**.

Vlad's legacy, particularly in his homeland of Romania, reflects the complex duality of his leadership. On one hand, he is celebrated as a **national hero** who fiercely defended Wallachia from foreign invaders, especially the Ottoman Empire. His harsh punishments, while brutal, were seen as necessary to maintain order and stability in a time of chaos. On the other hand, his reputation for cruelty and his association with **Dracula** have cemented his place in world history as a figure of **horror and tyranny**, embodying the darker aspects of **authoritarian rule**.

Vlad's leadership style has also had broader historical implications, influencing the way leaders are evaluated in times of **war, crisis**, or **internal instability**. His ability to wield **fear as a tool** for control shows that **brutal tactics** can be effective in the short term, but they can also **erode trust** and alienate allies. The lessons of Vlad's reign resonate in the stories of other authoritarian leaders throughout history, reminding us of the risks that come with ruling through terror and the fine line between **strong leadership** and **tyranny**.

In the end, Vlad's leadership style serves as a cautionary tale about the **consequences of fear-based rule**. His ability to seize and maintain power through **ruthlessness** has left an indelible mark on history, but it also underscores the importance of **moral leadership, fairness**, and **building alliances**. His reign highlights the enduring tension between **authority and ethics**, a dynamic that continues to shape leadership strategies and decisions to this day.

The importance of understanding historical context when analyzing leadership strategies

WHEN EVALUATING LEADERSHIP strategies, it is essential to consider the **historical context** in which they were developed and executed. The challenges, values, and expectations of different eras profoundly shape how leaders approach decision-making, governance, and control. **Leadership does not exist in a vacuum**—it is influenced by the **political, cultural, social**, and **economic realities** of the time. Without understanding these factors, it's easy to misinterpret or oversimplify the decisions and actions of historical figures.

1. Adapting Leadership to Unique Challenges

EVERY LEADER FACES challenges specific to their era, and the way they address those challenges reflects the context of their time. For example, Vlad the Impaler ruled during a period of **constant warfare,**

instability, and **foreign threats**. His reliance on fear, harsh punishments, and extreme measures can be better understood when considering the **violent and unpredictable environment** he lived in. Leaders of the past often had to contend with **limited resources**, fractured political systems, and **immediate threats** to their survival, which influenced their decision-making.

Without considering these factors, modern evaluations of leadership can seem unfair or misguided. What might seem brutal or unjust today may have been viewed as **necessary** and even **effective** in the context of the past. Understanding historical context allows for a more nuanced interpretation of leadership styles and the **constraints or pressures** leaders faced.

2. Shifting Values and Cultural Norms

LEADERSHIP STRATEGIES are often a reflection of the **values and norms** of a particular society. A leader's decisions, particularly those involving justice, authority, and power, are shaped by what was **culturally acceptable** at the time. Vlad's use of **impalement** and other severe punishments, for example, while horrifying by modern standards, were not unusual in his time. Public executions and harsh penalties were common methods for maintaining order and asserting authority across medieval Europe.

By examining leadership strategies through the lens of **historical values**, it becomes clear that what is perceived as **ruthless** or **inhumane** today may have been seen as effective governance in a society where **physical punishment** was an accepted norm. Leaders operate within the moral frameworks of their societies, and understanding those frameworks is crucial for interpreting their actions.

3. The Role of External Threats

HISTORICAL CONTEXT is especially important in understanding how leaders respond to **external threats**. Vlad the Impaler's reign occurred during a time when Wallachia was caught between powerful enemies, including the **Ottoman Empire** and **Hungary**. His leadership strategies were shaped by the need to **defend his territory** from foreign invasion and internal rebellion. His use of fear and brutality was not simply about maintaining control—it was about **survival** in a period when **constant warfare** and shifting alliances put smaller states like Wallachia at great risk.

In modern times, leaders may not face the same immediate physical threats, but understanding how external pressures—such as war, competition, or geopolitical challenges—shape leadership decisions is essential. Evaluating leaders in their **historical context** helps to clarify why certain strategies were pursued and whether they were the most appropriate responses to the threats of their time.

4. Comparing Leadership Across Eras

WHILE LEADERSHIP PRINCIPLES such as **vision, decisiveness,** and **influence** remain constant, the application of these principles changes dramatically depending on the era. Comparing the leadership of figures like Vlad the Impaler to modern leaders without accounting for **technological advances, diplomatic norms, and changes in governance structures** can lead to misleading conclusions. For example, leaders today have access to **diplomacy, global alliances, and advanced communication systems** that allow for more nuanced forms of control and influence.

Historical leaders often had fewer options and operated in more **isolated environments**, relying on force and visible displays of power to maintain control. By understanding these differences, modern evaluations of leadership can be more informed, offering insights into how **leadership evolves** over time.

5. Learning from Historical Leadership Without Imitation

UNDERSTANDING HISTORICAL context allows modern leaders to **learn from the past** without trying to **imitate** it. While figures like Vlad the Impaler offer lessons in **decisiveness, strategic thinking**, and the importance of authority, their methods may not translate well to today's world, where leadership is often more collaborative and driven by **ethical governance**. By placing historical leaders within their proper context, modern leaders can extract the **principles of leadership** that remain relevant, such as the need for **adaptability, resilience**, and **the careful balancing of power**, without adopting strategies that may no longer be effective or appropriate.

Conclusion

HISTORICAL CONTEXT is key to fully understanding and analyzing leadership strategies. Leaders throughout history have faced different challenges, operated under different cultural norms, and had access to different resources than today's leaders. By examining the **specific pressures** and **constraints** they faced, modern interpretations of leadership can be **more accurate, fair, and nuanced**. The ability to evaluate historical leadership in context allows us to learn from the past while **adapting the principles of leadership** to meet the needs and expectations of the present.

Appendix

1. Key Figures from Vlad the Impaler's Life

- **Vlad II Dracul**: Vlad the Impaler's father, ruler of Wallachia and member of the Order of the Dragon, which inspired the "Dracul" name. He was betrayed and killed by Wallachian boyars.

- **Radu the Handsome**: Vlad's younger brother, who aligned himself with the Ottoman Empire and ruled Wallachia after Vlad's imprisonment.

- **Mehmed II**: The Ottoman Sultan known as Mehmed the Conqueror, who led the Ottoman forces against Vlad and played a key role in his eventual downfall.

- **King Matthias Corvinus**: King of Hungary who initially supported Vlad but later imprisoned him to maintain political favor with European powers and the Papacy.

- **Stephen the Great**: Prince of Moldavia and Vlad's occasional ally in resisting Ottoman domination in Eastern Europe.

2. Timeline of Vlad the Impaler's Major Events

- **1448**: Vlad briefly becomes ruler of Wallachia for the first time but is quickly deposed.

- **1456**: Vlad returns to power in Wallachia, beginning his most significant period of rule.

- **1457**: Mass execution of boyars at the infamous Easter feast, solidifying Vlad's control over the nobility.

- **1462**: Vlad conducts the **Night Attack** against the Ottoman forces, leading to temporary success but eventual retreat.

- **1462**: Vlad is imprisoned by King Matthias Corvinus after seeking refuge in Hungary.

- **1475**: Vlad is released and reinstated as ruler of Wallachia with Hungarian support.

- **1476**: Vlad is killed in battle against Ottoman forces, marking the end of his reign.

3. Important Locations

- **Wallachia**: The region in modern-day Romania where Vlad ruled. Wallachia was a buffer state between the Ottoman Empire and Hungary, making it a frequent battleground.

- **Poenari Castle**: Vlad's primary fortress, located in a mountainous region of Wallachia, known for its strategic positioning and symbolic role in his defense.

- **Târgoviște**: The capital of Wallachia during much of Vlad's reign, where many of his brutal punishments and executions took place.

4. Key Battles and Military Tactics

- **Night Attack of 1462**: Vlad's famous guerrilla raid on the Ottoman camp, intended to assassinate Sultan Mehmed II. Though the assassination attempt failed, it demonstrated Vlad's strategic brilliance in asymmetric warfare.

- **Guerrilla Warfare**: Vlad employed guerrilla tactics, using his knowledge of the terrain and scorched-earth policies to exhaust and demoralize Ottoman forces.

- **Impalement**: Vlad's favored method of execution and intimidation, which he used to punish enemies, criminals, and traitors. Rows of impaled bodies served as both a military deterrent and a psychological weapon.

5. Vlad's Leadership and Governance

- **Ruling through fear**: Vlad maintained control over Wallachia by using fear and brutality to keep both internal enemies (like the boyars) and external threats (like the Ottomans) at bay.

- **Justice system**: Vlad's justice was swift and severe, with a focus on punishing crimes such as corruption, theft, and betrayal. His punishments, though extreme, were seen as effective at restoring order in a time of lawlessness.

- **Political isolation**: Despite his military successes, Vlad's methods alienated many potential allies, including Hungarian and European leaders, leading to his eventual political isolation and downfall.

6. Historical Interpretations of Vlad's Legacy

- **Romanian National Hero**: Vlad is celebrated in Romania as a protector of the nation, who defended Wallachia against Ottoman invasion and sought to maintain independence in a dangerous political environment.

- **The Dracula Myth**: Vlad's association with the fictional character Dracula, popularized by Bram Stoker's 1897 novel, has contributed to his image as a bloodthirsty villain in Western literature and culture, blending fact with gothic fiction.

- **Global Symbol of Ruthless Leadership**: Vlad has become a symbol of authoritarian rule, exemplifying both the effectiveness and dangers of leading through fear, control, and extreme punishment.

7. Lessons from Vlad's Reign

- **Decisiveness and Strategy**: Vlad's military tactics, especially his use of asymmetric warfare and knowledge of terrain, are valuable lessons in strategic thinking, especially when facing larger, more powerful forces.

- **The Limits of Fear-Based Rule**: While fear can be an effective tool for maintaining short-term control, Vlad's reign demonstrates the long-term risks of alienating allies and creating internal resentment.

- **Moral Boundaries in Leadership**: Vlad's reign shows the importance of balancing strength and decisiveness with ethical governance. Leaders who over-rely on brutality may achieve immediate success but risk isolation and eventual downfall.

8. Historical Sources and Further Reading

- **Primary Sources**: Contemporary accounts from Ottoman, Hungarian, and German chroniclers, who documented Vlad's reign, often in exaggerated or politically motivated terms.

- **Secondary Sources**: Modern historians' analyses of Vlad's leadership, including works that explore his role in defending Wallachia, his legacy in Romanian history, and his association with the Dracula myth.

  ○ **Florescu, Radu R., and Raymond T. McNally.** *Dracula: Prince of Many Faces*. Little, Brown and Company, 1989.

  ○ **Treptow, Kurt W.** *Vlad III Dracula: The Life and Times of the Historical Dracula*. Center for Romanian Studies, 2000.

9. Vlad in Popular Culture

- **Dracula Myth**: Vlad's name and reputation as a ruthless ruler were used as inspiration for Bram Stoker's *Dracula*, though the novel bears little resemblance to Vlad's actual life. The Dracula myth has since grown into a major component of gothic fiction and popular culture.

● **Tourism in Romania**: Vlad's legacy is a focal point for Romanian tourism, with sites such as **Bran Castle** (often mistakenly referred to as "Dracula's Castle") and **Poenari Castle** drawing visitors interested in both his historical life and the fictional Dracula story.